Biblical Truth
and
Modern Man

Biblical Truth and Modern Man

BRUCE D. RAHTJEN

ABINGDON PRESS
NASHVILLE AND NEW YORK

BIBLICAL TRUTH AND MODERN MAN

Copyright © 1968 by Abingdon Press

ISBN 0-687-03450-7

Library of Congress Catalog Card Number: 68-27625

SET UP, PRINTED, AND BOUND BY THE
PARTHENON PRESS, AT NASHVILLE,
TENNESSEE, UNITED STATES OF AMERICA

To my wife
Jeanne Hamilton Rahtjen

Preface

The first task of a new missionary in a foreign country is to establish communications with the people. He learns the language after a time, but finds that barriers to understanding still remain. He is translating Western concepts and thought-forms into nonwestern words, and is not understood. Communication begins when he understands the *culture* in which he is working. Then he can translate *ideas* rather than *words*.

So it is when an American picks up the Bible. With good English translations available, it appears easy to read. Before long, however, a culture gap shows up. How does a man whose language is scientific read a prescientific account of creation? How should twentieth-century man understand New Testament miracles?

What can we do with "history" which appears to contradict itself?

The purpose of this book is to chip away at the culture gap between the biblical world and modern man, so that the truth of the Bible can shine through. It is based on the unashamed assumption that the Bible *is* true, and that its truth is vital to modern man.

The material presented here has been drawn from seven years of Bible lectures in local churches and regional conferences. I have dealt with the issues most often raised in these Bible conferences. At many points my explanations have been sharpened by the searching and provocative questions of laymen. This book is intended not as a course in the Bible, but rather as a survey of what such a course would involve. I hope it may lead readers to organize study groups to begin serious study of the Bible. The bibliography will offer some guidance in that direction.

I am grateful to Dr. Charles Baughman, Rev. Daniel Evans, Rev. Donald Rahtjen, and William W. Sanders for their helpful suggestions; and to Marlous Haedt, Janice Manuel, Deanna Wright, and Barbara McClanahan for their secretarial help.

BRUCE D. RAHTJEN

Contents

9

1 The Book
Few People Know

The Bible may be the least read best seller of our day. Everyone seems to have at least one copy of it. Most people consider it the most important book ever written. Yet, even many people who attend church regularly seldom read the Bible.

Not long ago, a typical group of laymen gathered on a Sunday afternoon to begin a one-week study of the Bible. Most of them were church school teachers. All of them were looking forward to learning more about the Bible. The lecturer began by commenting on the good turnout. The planning committee had originally thought of starting the course on Saturday, but the hometown football team had a home game. It had been a good game, according to the Sunday morning headlines. How many had read about the game, the lecturer asked? Over half the group had. The football season was at its height. Even "Peanuts" in the Sunday morning comics had a football theme. How many of the group had read "Peanuts"? About two thirds of the hands went up. Then the speaker took his Bible from the lectern and opened it. How many of those present had read something in the Bible that day? Amid the red faces and embarrassed coughs, only a half-dozen hands went up. What an amazing revelation! This was not just a cross section of the congregation, but a group willing to devote several hours to serious Bible study. Even though they considered the Bible important and wanted to know more about it, they were not in the habit of reading it!

In former years our grandparents carried their Bibles to church on Sunday and read them regularly at home. Today we do neither. Protestants point to the Bible as the basis of their faith, but they depend on their ministers to read it for them and explain it to them. If our right to read and interpret Scripture for ourselves were threatened, we would fight for it. Why, then, since we do have it, don't we *use* it? The answer may lie within the Bible itself. Much as we respect and admire it, the Bible is difficult, puzzling, and sometimes unrewarding reading.

Part of the problem used to lie in the language. It

wasn't too long ago that the only readily available translation was the King James Version, first published in 1611. Since languages change rapidly in common use, a great deal has happened to English in the last 350 years. For one thing, all the *thees* and *thous* have dropped out, except in church. Even the minister has a terrible time keeping them straight, unless he writes out his pastoral prayers in advance. In the second place, many words have changed their meaning. For example, "preventing the dawn" sounds like quite an accomplishment, until you discover that "prevent" used to mean "precede." The word "let," which now means "to allow," used to mean "prevent." And so it goes! [1]

Now the Bible is easily available in any of several clear, modern translations.[2] However, several stumbling blocks to understanding it still remain. Even in the most modern language an angel is an angel and a demon is a demon. Who, in this day and age, can understand either one? In many ways the Bible seems to reflect a world quite different from ours. In the Bible men could leave the earth physically, with or without benefit of fiery chariot, and end up in heaven. Now astronauts have done the same thing, and they report that heaven is not up there. In biblical times men frequently reported conversations with God. Today he seems difficult, if not impossible, to reach. We read one story of the creation of man in the book of Genesis and quite another in our scientific textbooks. Then, to complicate matters further, we find that Genesis itself contains not one creation story, but two.[3]

The casual or occasional Bible reader is quickly impressed—not to say stunned—not only by the strangeness of the Bible's world, but also by the complexity and variety of its literature. Here are history, love poetry, battle songs, prayers, personal letters, hymns, and several other types of literature which defy classification. All the books are several centuries old, and they were written over a thousand-year period. No matter where he begins, the reader is overwhelmed by unfamiliar places, people, and events.

The Bible seems to overdo everything. Why are there four Gospels instead of one, when they all tell the same basic story? Why are there two separate Old Testament histories, Kings and Chronicles? Even some of the books themselves seem to be "too much." Who can follow all the detailed descriptive passages in Leviticus? Who understands all the wild imagery in Revelation? How did the erotic passages in Ezekiel and the Song of Solomon ever slip by the censors?

Unless you know the Bible well, it is difficult even to know where to begin reading it. You can start with Genesis, of course, and just begin working your way through. Chances are, though, you'll begin slowing down about Exodus 25 and will give up completely before you finish Leviticus. If you begin with the New Testament, Matthew goes fairly well. Then when you get to Mark, the story begins all over again. By the time you get to Luke, you are reading some passages for the third time. Even if you skip on to Paul's letters, you find that they are confusing, too. We know who the Romans were, but why did Paul write them a letter? Who were the Colossians and Thessalonians? Without a program it is difficult to identify the players and nearly impossible to sort out the important ideas.

The fact is that without outside help it is very difficult to read the Bible with real understanding. It is, of course, possible to get *some* help from the Bible just from one reading of one section. However, serious study for lasting gain requires careful planning and a great deal of hard work.

At this point I propose a short quiz to sample your knowledge of the Bible. Although it is too short and too general to prove much, it may give us a basis for discussion. Take a pencil and a piece of paper and jot down your answers to the following questions:

1. How many disciples did Jesus have?
2. How many of them can you name?
3. How would you go about checking your answer quickly?
4. Where would you look to find the Ten Commandments?
5. What is the longest book of the Bible?
6. Can you name a book of the Bible which has only one chapter?
7. What kind of fruit did Eve eat in the garden?

8. How many of each kind of animal did Noah take into the Ark?
9. What is described in I Timothy as the "root of evil"?
10. What is the "curse of Ham"?

If you have all your answers jotted down, let's look at the questions one at a time. Chances are you knew that Jesus had twelve disciples. Almost everyone has learned that in Sunday school. On the other hand, you probably couldn't name even half of them correctly. Most people begin with Matthew, Mark, Luke, and John. If you did that, you were 50 percent wrong already! Matthew and John were disciples of Jesus, but Mark and Luke were not.

Question 3 tests both your knowledge of the Bible and your ability to look up things you don't know. If you know where to look for the listing of the Twelve (Matthew 10, Mark 3, Luke 11, Acts 1), fine. If not, you will need to use a concordance or a Bible dictionary.[4] The answer to question 4 could be either Exodus 20 or Deuteronomy 5. A slightly different version of the decalogue is found in Exodus 34. The answer to number 5 is the book of Psalms, with 150 chapters. Question 6 has several correct answers. One-chapter books are Obadiah, Philemon, II John, III John, and Jude. Questions 5 and 6 test your familiarity with the whole Bible. Many people who know one or two books quite well concentrate on them and neglect the rest of the Bible.

16

How many correct answers do you have so far? One or two would be about average. Three would be excellent. Four or more right answers probably means you don't really need to read the rest of this book because you have already done considerable serious Bible study.

The first seven questions were designed to see how much information you have on the Bible. The last three were designed to show up *mis*information. Did you say it was an apple Eve ate and shared with her husband? Read Genesis 2:17. It was the fruit of the tree of knowledge of good and evil. The "apple" idea probably originated with artists who didn't know what the fruit of knowledge would look like. Question 8 is another tricky one. If you answered "two animals of each kind" you were only partly right. According to Genesis 6:19, it was two of each, but Genesis 7:2 says *seven* of each clean (i.e., edible) species. Was your answer to question 9 "Money is the root of all evil"? If so, read I Timothy 6:10. The source of evil is not money itself, but the *love* of it. Question 10 deals with a nonexistent curse. Many people point to a curse on Ham, presumably the father of the black and brown races, as an explanation for the race problems of recent years. However, the curse they refer to was actually directed at Ham's son Canaan, who was the ancestor of the Canaanites (Genesis 9:25).

There are many false impressions in general circulation today about the Bible. Given a chance, the Bible itself can correct these false assumptions. However, some of these ideas can give us a perverted understanding of the Bible before we ever begin to read it. One of the most dangerous mistakes we can make is to allow the Bible to take the place of God. Anything which receives the honor and respect due only to God is an idol, no matter how holy it may be. The Bible is a means by which we may know God in order to be able to serve him. If we make the Bible an end in itself, we turn it into an idol. We have to be careful to remember that while the Bible is the Word of God, it is not God himself. Therefore, we should avoid attributing to it such divine characteristics as inerrancy or absolute power. It is one thing to attribute these characteristics to God. It is something else again to claim them for the Bible.

Nowhere does the Bible claim that it is inerrant. Nowhere does it claim for itself absolute knowledge or absolute power over human life. By what non-biblical authority, then, can we regard it in this way? We should give the Bible the greatest respect as a revelation of God, but we must avoid idolatry by remembering that it is also a human document.

As soon as we say that the Bible is both the Word of God and the work of men, we have raised the question of "inspiration." As Christians, we believe that the Bible is inspired of God, but we are not always sure just what that means.

Some people believe that God actually dictated the Bible word by word and line by line to the authors of the various books. As we read through the next few chapters, we shall see that this view seems to raise more theological questions than it answers. Furthermore, this sort of inspiration is not claimed by the Bible itself, but is a part of *human tradition.*

On the opposite end of the spectrum, we find people who define "inspiration" in the Bible in the same way that they would define it in any other great piece of literature. "Sure, I think the Bible is inspired," they may say, "but I think that Shakespeare's plays were inspired too. The Bible is just one great book out of many in world literature."

I would suggest that the truth of biblical inspiration lies between these two extremes. God has taken the initiative in revealing himself to men, and men have responded to this revelation by recording it in written form. The Bible is not a record of man's search for God, but rather the record of God's search for man, and this distinction is important. On the other hand, since the Bible was produced by man, it contains an element of human misunderstanding and confusion.

Perhaps the best place to look for a definition of biblical inspiration is the Bible itself. Surprisingly, the subject is dealt with specifically only in II Timothy 3:16: "Every scripture which is inspired by God [God-spirited] is also profitable for teaching, for reproof, for correction, and for training in righteousness, that the man of God may be complete, prepared for every good work." [5] Thus, the Bible is set apart from other literature by the special presence of the *Spirit of God* within it. Therefore it has a special relationship to man. No other book contains or reveals God's spirit in quite the same way. We therefore refer to the Bible as the Word of God, and we set its books aside in a special category or "canon" of scripture.

Before we go any further in our study of the meaning of the Bible for twentieth-century man, perhaps we should pause to see how and when it was written, and how the concept of a biblical canon came into being.

2   How Did
the Bible Happen?

The Old Testament

How can a *book* be called "the Word of God"? The idea doesn't sound strange to us, because we have grown up with the Bible. Historically, however, the whole idea of "Scripture," or revelation by means of a book, is rather a recent development in Hebrew religion.

From a very early period the Hebrews believed that God revealed himself in personal encounter. Furthermore, there were some men who were spokesmen for God. The word "prophet," which means "spokesman," was used to describe Aaron in Exodus 4:16. Moses was to tell Aaron what to say, and Aaron would be Moses' spokesman or prophet.

During the history of the Hebrews, God called many prophets to proclaim his message. Moses, Nathan, Amos, Isaiah, and Jeremiah all began their preaching by saying "Thus says the Lord. . . ." It was taken for granted that when God spoke to his people he did so through the mouth of a prophet. The idea that a book might be the Word of God began in the seventh century B.C., in a rather interesting way.

The Law

In 621, King Josiah began an extensive renovation of the Jerusalem Temple (II Kings 22). In the process, one of the workmen discovered an ancient scroll in an out-of-the-way corner. The workman took it to the high priest, who in turn took it to the king.

When the king read the book, he and his advisors were horrified. The scroll claimed to be the law of God, dating back to the time of Moses. After an impressive list of commandments, it promised prosperity to the nation if these laws were followed, but disaster if they were ignored. Since the book had just been found, few of the laws had ever been followed. If this book was not really a revelation of God's will, then there was nothing to worry about. On the other hand, if the book was what it claimed to be, the king, the high priest, and the people were all in trouble.

Since the prophets were best acquainted with the

ways of God the book was sent to a prophetess named Huldah.[1] She declared that the book was the Word of God, but added a word of comfort. Since the book had just been discovered, she said, God would not hold the people responsible for what had been done in the past.

In a real sense, Huldah's judgment on this book changed the whole course of Hebrew religion. Previously, God's revelation had come by word of mouth. Now his law had been equated with a particular scroll. From that time on, the importance of the prophets began to diminish, and the Hebrews became more and more a people dependent on scripture, or written law.

The book found in the temple was called simply "The Book of the Law" or "The Book of the Covenant." As nearly as we can tell, it consisted of what is now Deuteronomy, chapters 12–26. No one knows just when it was written. It was an old scroll when it was found, and the ideas in it were older than the scroll itself.[2]

The acceptance of Deuteronomy as written law raised several important questions. For a long time the Hebrews' lives had been governed by laws handed from one generation to the next in oral tradition. Some of these laws had come from the time of the Exodus. Others had been added to the collection during the course of Hebrew history. If part of the law had been committed to writing now and was considered to be scripture, shouldn't the rest of the law now be written down and treated in the same way?

23

On this basis many of the oral traditions which the Hebrews had received from their ancestors were drawn together and written down. By 400 B.C. the books which we know as the Pentateuch—Genesis, Exodus, Leviticus, Numbers, and Deuteronomy—had been completed in their present form and declared to be scripture.[3]

Perhaps at this point we should say a few words about oral tradition. This is a term used to refer to material which is not written down, but handed on by word of mouth alone. Generally, we don't put much stock in oral tradition today. Maybe you have played a party game called "Gossip." One person writes down a fairly long sentence and then whispers it in the ear of the person next to him. This person whispers it to the person next to him, and so on all the way around the circle. When all have passed the sentence along, the last person writes the sentence as he heard it. Then this sentence is compared with what was originally written. The game always turns out the same way. In the process of going from one ear to the next, the sentence is always changed. For this reason many people today are troubled when they hear that ideas were passed along in oral tradition before they were written down. This is especially true when we are talking about the Bible. If these ideas were in oral tradition, how do we know they weren't changed a great deal from the time they originated?

The answer is that oral tradition in the biblical

period was much more reliable than we might think. The people who used it could not read and write. Anyone who cannot read and write depends on oral tradition a great deal. When he has memorized something he knows it by heart and will not allow anybody to change it. In order to prove this point to yourself, try reading a bedtime story to a child who has not yet started school. As you read a tale which the child knows well, try to change a few words or to skip a page. You will discover at once that you have a rebellion on your hands! The child knows the story by heart and is not going to let you change even a single word of it. Once he learns to read and write and does not have to depend on his memory so much, then his attitude will soften. Since the Hebrews had to depend on their memory during the period of oral tradition, the ideas were handed from one generation to another with no accidental changes.

The Prophets

Acceptance of the books of the Pentateuch as the Word of God caused another problem. For a long time the words of the great prophets had been considered to be inspired by God. Amos and Jeremiah had spoken for God, just as Moses did. Now the traditions connected with Moses had been put into written form and were declared to be "scripture." But by this time, the sermons of the great prophets were also in written form. Since these books contained the revelations of

God to and through the prophets, shouldn't they also be considered to be scripture? Obviously, the suggestion was logical, and it quickly gained popular support. Some of the books of prophetic sermons were used as scripture quite early in certain areas. As time went on, the acceptance of this idea spread far and wide.

These prophetic books had been collected and edited by disciples of the prophets. Most of the great prophets gathered around them groups of disciples, much like the followers of Jesus. As a prophet preached, his sermons were remembered and repeated by his disciples. Eventually, these sermons were written down. Included with them were stories about the prophet's life, and even the better sermons of some of his followers. Since the books were compiled long before they were considered to be scripture, there was no attempt to sort out the prophet's preaching from his disciples' additions.[4]

In this way four scrolls of the "prophets" were produced. All of them were approximately the same length. The four scrolls were Isaiah (now known to consist of three separate books), Jeremiah, Ezekiel, and "The Twelve." The scroll of The Twelve contained what we now refer to as the "minor prophets." These brief books are called the minor prophets only because of their length, not because of their importance. Some of the so-called minor prophets—such as Amos, Hosea, and Micah—may be more "major" in their importance than the so-called major prophet Ezekiel.

Once these four books of prophecy were accepted as

scripture, another problem arose. The books of the Pentateuch told the story of the relationship between God and his people from the creation of the world until the death of Moses (*ca.* 1300-1250 B.C.). The four scrolls of the prophets began with the first sermon of Amos, in 750 B.C. This meant that the newly defined canon of scripture had a 500-year gap from the death of Moses to the beginning of Amos' ministry. But one of the most important elements in Hebrew theology was the unbroken relationship in history between God and his people. Therefore, the Hebrews could hardly allow a 500-year historical gap in their sacred writings. In order to make the scriptures complete, it was necessary to include the history of the period from Joshua to Amos. This history was duly compiled and added to the canon of scripture in four books: Joshua, Judges, Samuel, and Kings. (The division of Samuel and Kings into two books each took place at a much later time.) These four books of history were known as the "former prophets." The four books of true prophecy were called the "latter prophets." These former and latter prophets were canonized about 200 B.C.

The Hebrew historical books contain history which was written in a rather unusual way. Most history is written either backward or forward. Backward history is written by a writer who, from his own historical perspective, digs back into the past to find out what happened before his own time. Forward history is written by someone who keeps a record of events day by day, as in a diary. The history of the Hebrews from Joshua to Amos was written neither backward nor forward, but from the middle toward both ends.

When David became king of all the Hebrews, he established Jerusalem as a central capital. His new central government taxed all the people and brought the tax moneys to Jerusalem where they were disbursed as needed. This meant that records of taxes had to be kept. Usually, when a nation begins to keep careful fiscal records, it begins to keep other written records as well.[5] Therefore, David was the first Hebrew ruler to have royal scribes and secretaries.[6] These men were instructed to keep a record of all that went on in David's court. As we read these records today, we feel that perhaps the scribes took David a bit too literally. They included not only all the important governmental matters, but also a number of personal details, such as David's relation with Bathsheba. History has been enriched by the former materials, and American movie producers have been enriched by the latter.

After the period of David's reign, those who were interested in the events of his period could get information from the records kept in the palace. During the reign of Solomon, his successor, equally careful historical records were kept. When the Hebrew nation divided into the twin kingdoms of Israel and Judah at the death of Solomon, separate records were kept in the court of each king. We have references in the books of Kings to "the book of the acts of the kings of Judah" and "the book of the acts of the kings of Israel." Although those who wanted to know what had happened during and after the reign of King David were able to find records to satisfy their curiosity, those who wanted records from the time of Saul and earlier were disappointed. No records had been kept during Saul's reign or during the period of the Judges.

Because of general interest in these periods, stories of what had happened during the reign of Saul were compiled from oral traditions and later written sources. Similarly, the story of the period of the Judges was reconstructed. Little by little, the historical records of early Hebrew times were pushed back into the time of the Patriarchs. The history from the conquest to the time of David was written backward, and the history from the time of David onward was written forward. Thus, we can say that this history from the Conquest to Amos was written toward both ends from the middle.

The "Writings"

After the canonization of the former and latter prophets in 200 B.C., the Hebrew Bible remained unchanged for nearly three centuries. During this period, however, there were certain books which were given a special place of honor in Hebrew usage. The most important and most popular was the book of Psalms.

The Psalms were written over a period of several centuries, and they were often used in Hebrew worship. Because they were used in worship in synagogue and temple alike, people came to look at them in a new light. Some began to think of the Psalms as having the same authority as scripture. As time went on, other books became very popular and were used in synagogue services, if not in the temple. As these books grew in popularity, the religious authorities tended to recognize them as a part of scripture. Among the most popular books in this group were Proverbs, Ecclesiastes, Job, the Song of Solomon, and the Wisdom of Solomon. Finally, these Writings were canonized as a third section of the Bible, but not until about A.D. 90. About fifteen new books were accepted and the same number (the Apocrypha) were rejected.[7]

The New Testament

The Christian church never intended to have any separate scripture of its own. This sounds strange to us today, because we take the New Testament very much for granted. But as far as the early church was concerned, the Bible had already been written.

In the New Testament itself there are several references to the Old Testament as scripture. In the Sermon on the Mount Jesus says, "Think not that I have come to abolish the law and the prophets; I have come not to abolish them but to fulfill them" (Matthew 5:17). "The law and the prophets" is a reference to the five books of Moses and the eight books of prophecy.

In the parable of the rich man and Lazarus (Luke 16:19-31), the rich man asks for permission to return from the dead to tell his father and his brothers what their fate will be if they follow in his footsteps. The answer is, "No, they have Moses and the prophets." Again, the reference is to the first two sections of the Hebrew Bible.

The church's dependence on the Old Testament as its scripture was not the only reason for the feeling that no new scripture was required. A second reason was the belief that the return of Jesus, the final judgment, and the end of history would come almost any day. Since the end was almost at hand, there would be no point in writing an account of Jesus and his ministry. Christians could not afford to waste time in writing or reading books. Their responsibility was to reach as many people as possible in the short time that remained, by means of preaching.

Because of these two factors, it was a long time before any Christian literature was produced. As nearly as we can tell from scholarly research, Jesus was born sometime between 7 and 4 B.C.[8] He began his ministry at about the age of 30, and his ministry was approximately one year in length.[9] This means that his resurrection and the beginning of the church took place between A.D. 24 and 27. The earliest book in the New Testament, I Thessalonians, was written about A.D. 51. The earliest Gospel, the Gospel according to Mark, is dated about A.D. 64. The latest book in the New Testament, II Peter, dates from about A.D. 150. This means that the literature of the New Testament was produced over a period of about a century, with the earliest material at least 25 years later than any events of Jesus' life. Furthermore, the earliest Gospel is about 40 years later than any of the events it describes. For some 40 years, the stories about who Jesus was and what he said circulated in oral tradition. Even though we would give almost anything to have these materials in written form, there is no way that they can be reconstructed today. We wish that the early Christians had put their memories of Jesus into writing much earlier, but we can understand why they did not. Since there was such a long period between the beginning of the church and the writing of the New Testament literature, we might ask how these books ever came to be written at all. Historians today, looking back on the first and second centuries, can see several situations which brought them into being.

The Letters of Paul

The very earliest New Testament literature resulted from the unexpected success of Paul's Gentile mission. The Jerusalem church leaders apparently never intended to spread the gospel very far beyond Palestine. Since the end of the world was expected soon, there wasn't time to preach the good news to the whole world. The man who broke this pattern was Paul, who refused to abide by *any* restrictions in his missionary work. Paul went first to the Syrians and the people of Asia Minor. This was out of line with the plans of the

Jerusalem church, but Paul did not stop even there. In response to a call received in a dream, Paul went to Macedonia in northern Greece and began to organize new churches.

Under Paul's leadership, the church spread rapidly throughout Greece. In town after town, Paul gathered small groups of people and organized them into churches. After spending just a few weeks or months in one place, Paul's restless energy would drive him on to another town to gather still another group of Christians. This, of course, left the first group with no leadership. Paul's converts were able to keep the church going by themselves and even to increase the membership through evangelism. However, they had depended on Paul for help in problems of theology. Many questions arose in his absence which the church members were unable to answer. Furthermore, without any theological guidance they easily slipped into former practices which were less than Christian.

Consequently, Paul wrote a great many letters to his former congregations. In some cases the letters were answers to questions which the people had sent messengers to ask. For example, I Thessalonians answers questions concerning the Final Judgment. The Thessalonians were concerned about the baptized Christians who had already died. What would happen to these people, they wondered, when Christ returned? Could they attain resurrection from the dead, although they had died before the day of resurrection? Paul reassured them that the all-powerful Ruler of history could be depended upon to take care of those who believed and trusted in him, whether they were living or dead.

A second problem of the Thessalonians concerned those who wanted to stop working because they thought the end of the world was near. All the members of the church, they suggested, should pool their resources, and then they could all live on this shared wealth until Christ returned. That way, no one would have to spend time in working, but all could spend their full time in preaching the gospel. Paul's answer was brief and to the point: "Those who don't work don't eat!"

Sometimes the letters of Paul were not responses to requests for information, but were his outraged reactions to reports of trouble. I Corinthians is an excellent example of Paul's reaction to disturbing reports from one of his churches. He begins by telling the Corinthians that he has heard of divisions and fighting within the church. He then goes on to discuss their false doctrines, their immorality, and their misunderstanding of the nature and purpose of the Lord's Supper.

Although there were many things in Paul's letters that made the churches smart under his lash, they realized that these letters were theological and literary gems, not to be thrown away but to be cherished. Therefore, many of them were kept by the churches which had received them. From time to time the letters were read to the congregations in the same way that the

Old Testament scrolls were read. If Christianity in Europe had not spread more rapidly than leadership could be provided for the new churches, Paul's letters would not have been written. Thus, the unexpected success of Paul's Gentile mission provided us with nearly one third of our present New Testament literature.[10]

The Gospels

A second situation which occasioned the writing of New Testament literature was the passing of the first generation of Christians. About A.D. 64, the Emperor Nero commanded that all Christians in the city of Rome be put to death. According to tradition, both Simon Peter and Paul were then in Rome and were executed at Nero's order. Some Christians managed to escape the Roman soldiers and hid in a series of damp limestone caves under the city, near the Tiber River. Here in the catacombs they were able to avoid Nero's soldiers and thus survive until the persecution was over.

The leader of the Christians in the catacombs appears to have been a man named John Mark.[11] Tradition tells us that he was a young man in the city of Jerusalem at the time that Jesus was put to death, and that the Jerusalem church met in his mother's home in Jerusalem, after Pentecost. John Mark was a nephew of Barnabas who was a companion of Paul, and he accompanied Paul and Barnabas on at least one missionary journey. Sometime in the 60's, Mark went to Rome.

Tradition tells us that he was a companion of Simon Peter there, translating Peter's sermons from Aramaic into the Greek spoken by the common people.

Mark realized that forty years had passed since the death and resurrection of Jesus. The Second Coming had not yet taken place, and no one seemed to know exactly when it would be. Many of the people who had known Jesus had already died. Most of the twelve disciples and many of their followers had died during the past forty years. Two whole generations had been born since the day of Pentecost. There were fewer and fewer people who could answer questions like, What did Jesus really say about life after death? Mark decided that the time had come to prepare a written record for another generation of Christians, who had not known Jesus. Drawing on all his resources, he wrote a story of Jesus' ministry, teachings, death, and resurrection. In writing his story of Jesus, Mark developed a new literary form— the Gospel—which was later used by a number of other Christian writers. The term "gospel" means "good news." The good news of which Mark wrote was what God had done in Jesus Christ. It was not the good news, or gospel, of Mark but the gospel of God. Mark simply wrote his version, or account, of it. Therefore, we refer to this book as *the* Gospel *according* to Mark."

Later on, a number of other writers wrote their own versions of God's good news. The Gospel according to Matthew was probably written between A.D. 80 and 90 as an instruction manual for newly converted Jewish

Christians. If you look closely at Matthew, you can see many elements calculated to lead the reader from Judaism to Christianity. For example, Jesus is clearly shown to be a successor to Moses. Read through Matthew and see how many parallels you can find between the life of Jesus and the life of Moses. On the basis of these parallels Matthew shows that the Sermon on the Mount has taken the place of the Ten Commandments.

The Gospel according to Luke was another book written because of the passing of the first generation of Christians. Luke addressed his book to a man named Theophilus, who was apparently a potential convert. Theophilus wanted to become a Christian but was puzzled by contradictory reports of the life and meaning of Jesus. Luke, a former companion of Paul, decided to write "an orderly account" of the gospel for his friend Theophilus (Luke 1:1-4). The Gospel according to Luke is only one volume of a two-volume work. The Acts of the Apostles shows that it is volume two (see Acts 1:1). The Gospel ends with the account of Jesus' resurrection. The book of Acts begins with the Ascension and then tells the story of the Christian church until the time of Paul's death in Rome.

If you look carefully at Matthew, Mark, and Luke, you will see that much of the text of the three is identical, word-for-word. In some places Matthew and Luke agree against Mark. In other places all three have quite different readings. These similarities and differences are puzzling, to say the least.

Scholars now know that Matthew and Luke both copied a good bit from Mark. In addition, both of them used another source, consisting mainly of the sayings of Jesus. No scholar has ever seen a copy of the source which they used, although we keep hoping that some day it will turn up as the Dead Sea Scrolls did.[12] In addition to Mark and this common source, Matthew and Luke each had a collection of private sources. These private sources explain the rather different birth and resurrection stories found in Matthew and Luke.

The Gospel according to John was written about the end of the first century. Like the first three Gospels, it was written because of the disappearance of the first generation of Christians. Because it was intended for a much wider audience than any of the other Gospels, it was written in terms which could be easily understood by anyone who had been educated in Greek or Roman schools, as we shall see below.

Later New Testament Books

We have seen that Paul's letters were written because of the success of the Gentile mission, and the four Gospels and the book of Acts were written because of the passing of the first generation. Three other books in the New Testament were written because of the official persecution of Christians by the Roman government. Since the Mediterranean Sea was a Roman lake, there was no place for Christians to hide from a Roman persecution. There was no place to escape, because the lands outside of the Roman empire were inhabited by Goths, Vandals, and Huns, who were no more pleasant than Roman persecutors. On several occasions after the time of Nero, Roman Emperors decreed that all Christians in the Empire should be put to death. When this happened, tracts were written for the persecuted Christians, giving them advice and offering them some hope. The books of Revelation, Hebrews, and I Peter were written as a result of Roman persecution. Read through I Peter and the first part of Hebrews to see if you can find references to these persecutions.

There are several books in the New Testament for which we have not yet accounted. All of them were written in order to settle problems which had arisen within the Christian church. Some of these problems dealt with doctrines, others had to do with the way in which the life of the church was carried on. All the books which have not been mentioned so far fall into this general category of "books written to settle disputes." These would include I and II Timothy, Titus, II Peter, Jude, James, I, II, and III John, and possibly Ephesians.

Sometimes we can read one of these books and see quite clearly what the dispute was. For example, I John 4 says that all traveling preachers should be questioned before being allowed to preach. If they said that Jesus Christ had come in the *flesh* then their theology was all right. Otherwise, they were not to be allowed to preach.

The point at issue here was the theology of Docetism. The Docetics said that Jesus was not human. Since God was completely good and men were evil, God could not really have become a man. Jesus, therefore, was only pretending to be human. This, of course, denied the reality of the Incarnation. Therefore, it was declared to be a heresy, and several passages in the New Testament were written to deny it. At the end of the Fourth Gospel, Jesus was shown to be completely human by the fact that he suffered from thirst and his side bled when pierced by a spear.[13] The reason for stressing the fact that Jesus was born of a human mother (in Matthew 1 and Luke 2) is to show that he was a human being. Today the docetic heresy is not popular, since people are more apt to admit that Jesus was human and deny that he was the Son of God. Therefore, the birth stories are sometimes used today to prove that Jesus was the Son of God—a complete reversal of their original purpose.

The New Testament Canon

Now that we have seen how the individual books of the New Testament came to be written, let us see how they were gathered together into their present form. Most of the New Testament writers probably did not know that they were writing scripture. They saw their books as responses to specific historical needs. Today, looking back on the first century, we can see the hand of God at work in the writing of these books. However,

40

we have to remember that hindsight is always 20/20, giving a perspective not available at the time an event takes place.

The first collection of individual New Testament books into a body of literature came at the end of the first century A.D. Sometime after the book of Acts was published, a messenger was sent out to retrace the journeys of Paul. He visited all the churches listed in the book of Acts as places where he had worked. In each case, the same question was asked: "Do you have a letter which Paul wrote to your church?" In each case the answer was "yes." All these letters were collected by the messenger and taken back to his home, probably in Ephesus. There they were collected into one scroll, which very quickly became popular among the churches in Europe and Asia Minor.

Not too many years later, someone produced a scroll which contained four Gospels. Some scholars suggest that this was done in order to make the Fourth Gospel popular. Matthew, Mark, and Luke were already well accepted by the time the Fourth Gospel was written. If you have forgotten how different the Fourth Gospel is from the three others, go back and compare just two or three chapters of each. John picks up many of the ideas and categories of Greek philosophy. In addition, most of the teachings of Jesus are recorded in dialogues very much like those used by the Greek philosopher Plato. Apparently, someone collected the three most popular Gospels in the same scroll with John. He began with

Matthew, which is the most Jewish Gospel. It was written by a Jewish Christian for Jewish Christians. Mark, the second Gospel on the scroll, was written by a Jewish Christian for Jews and Gentiles alike. It was written in Rome, and Mark was not sure exactly who his audience would be. The Gospel according to Luke was written by a Gentile for a Gentile, but Luke used Jewish ideas and terminology. Often, though, he had to stop and explain these Jewish terms to his friend Theophilus. Luke's problem in using Jewish terms to express the Gospel to a Roman points up the value of the Fourth Gospel. Anyone can read the Fourth Gospel without taking a short course in Judaism. He doesn't have to know who Abraham, Isaac, Jacob, Moses, and David were in order to read and understand the message of salvation which John presents. This meant that the Fourth Gospel could be used all over Europe, with people who had never heard of the Old Testament or the Hebrews. As you read through the four Gospels, you go from Matthew, which is quite Jewish, to John, which contains many more Greek ideas and concepts.

By the middle of the second century, the scroll of Paul's letters and the scroll of the four Gospels had become very popular. Many churches had both scrolls and used them often in their services of worship. In addition, some of the other books of the New Testament were used in various churches. There was no agreement, however, as to exactly what books should be included as Christian scripture. By the end of the second century, there were several dozen Gospels, at least a dozen books of Revelation, several books of Acts, and hundreds of letters.[14] Someone had to decide whether the church was going to have a Testament of its own and, if so, which books would be included.

About A.D. 140 a heretic named Marcion made the first list of books that should be in the New Testament. Marcion's Bible was very strange. It left out the Old Testament entirely. Furthermore, the only Gospel accepted was that of Luke. Marcion removed sections of the Gospel that he didn't care for and made a selection of a few of the letters of Paul. Even these were edited severely in terms of Marcion's own theology.[15]

Very few accepted Marcion's canon as the final answer. However, church leaders began to realize that they must have a definite list of New Testament books. Otherwise, there would be no end to the number of books that would be accepted as scripture by some churches. Finally, it was decided that each Bishop would have the right to determine, for his own diocese, what was in the New Testament. For a long time this was the accepted system. Finally, after the council of Nicaea (A.D. 325), the list of the Bishop of Rome was accepted by most Christians. This was the list of 27 books which we have in our New Testament today.[16]

Now, having looked briefly at how the Bible came to be, we should turn to the question of its truth. Perhaps the best way to begin is to define the word "truth" as it is generally used and as it relates to the Bible.

43

3   Facts and Fiction

"What is truth?" Pontius Pilate asked Jesus (John 18:38). Though often bypassed and ignored, this is one of the most important questions in the entire New Testament. Before we can discuss the question, Is the Bible true? we have to agree on a definition of "truth." And yet, how often we ask the question or try to answer it without stopping to define this critical word!

Truth is not a simple concept. Look the word up in a dictionary and the number of different definitions will amaze you. "True" may mean "faithful" or "loyal." In this sense, a man is said to be true to his friends. The word may mean "reliable"; for example, a thermometer gives a true indication of temperature. Another definition is "correct," meaning "not containing errors." In another context, "true" can mean "genuine" or "properly so called." A "true heir," on the other hand, is one who has a legitimate or rightful claim. Or the word "true" may mean "conforming to an original," as in a true likeness or picture.

When you ask the question, "Is the Bible true? what are you really asking? Are you inquiring whether the Bible is faithful to God? Are you referring to the presence or absence of errors in the book? Are you asking whether or not the Bible is meaningful?

It is obvious that before dealing with the truth of the Bible we have to define our terms. Perhaps the most common use or meaning of the word "true" in everyday usage is "factual" or "correct." However, when we apply this definition to the truth of the Bible, we get into difficulties.

Some time ago, I was giving a series of lectures on the Bible in a small Midwestern church. One member of the congregation seemed to have real doubts about my presentation. As soon as she could, she asked a question which seemed to be in the minds of many other listeners. "Do you believe," she asked, "that the Bible contains fiction?" As I thought about the question for a moment, many others in the audience leaned forward intently. Obviously, my answer to this question would tell them how much they could depend on *anything* I might say about the Bible.

45

The answer I gave was not the one the group wanted to hear. I had to say, in all honesty, that I do think the Bible contains fiction. At once a buzz went through the group, and I could see about a dozen faces simply turn off. Their worst fears were realized! How could any minister say that the Bible contains fiction? Where was my evidence? My answer was to direct their attention to II Samuel 12.

In this passage, David had just received a visit from the prophet Nathan. Nathan came to see the King when he heard about David's marriage to Bathsheba, a very beautiful woman whom David loved at first sight. He wanted to marry her at once, but unfortunately she already had a husband. However, since Uriah was a captain in David's army, he was sent, at the King's request, to "the forefront of the hottest battle" where he met a speedy death.[1] Then David volunteered to console the widow, and married Bathsheba.

When Nathan heard about the marriage, he went to the King and asked his help in settling a dispute. His story dealt with two men who presumably lived in David's kingdom. One of them was very wealthy, having a herd of many sheep and goats. The other man had only one small ewe lamb. This lamb was something of a family pet, since it ate and slept with the children. One day the rich man had a visitor. According to the code of the nomad, he had to prepare a meal for the stranger.[2] Instead of killing one of his own sheep, he

46

took the lamb of the poor man and served it up to his guest.

When Nathan finished the story, he asked David what he thought of the man who had done this deed. Naturally, David was furious. He said that the rich man would have to pay back the loss four times over, and then he should be put to death for his crime. Of course, David wanted to know who the man was. The prophet stared at the King long and hard before he replied with a cold smile, "You are the man! Suddenly, David realized that the story was not about two of his subjects and their sheep at all. The story was about the King, Uriah, and Bathsheba!

The reason that I brought up this story of Nathan and David as an illustration of fiction in the Bible is because Nathan's story was *not literally true*. As a matter of fact, Nathan made the story up out of whole cloth. It was fiction, pure and simple, and yet it appears in the Bible!

On the other hand, even though Nathan's story was fiction, it was still true. The fact that the prophet made it up for the occasion did not change its truth in any way. The question, then, is not whether the story is *fiction*, but whether or not it contains *truth*. The *meaning* of the story is a great deal more important than its *factualness*.

Suppose that David had tried to get around Nathan's story by challenging its literal truth. Suppose he had said, "Nathan, you have just told me a story which may or may not be true. We are going to search my kingdom to find out whether or not these two men exist. If we discover that there is a man in my kingdom who has done what you have described, we will certainly punish him. But if we find out that your story has been made up and is therefore not true, then you will be thrown into prison for telling me a lie!"

What would Nathan's reply to the king have been under these circumstances? He would probably have said, "O King, you seem to be ducking the issue! Whether or not these two men exist makes no difference. I told you this story to get you to see the real meaning of what you had done. The story is true, and you recognize its truth. Whether it is literally correct or not makes no difference at all."

If the literal factualness of Nathan's story had nothing to do with its meaning, then the Bible *can* contain fiction and still be meaningful and true. It appears, then, that the question of "truth" versus "fiction" in the Bible is not as simple as it might seem at first. For example, what happens to these categories of truth and fiction when we look at Jesus' parables?

All Christians would agree that the parables are true. But what is the relationship between their truth and their historicity? Did all the stories Jesus told describe things that had actually happened? Was there really a woman who swept the house all day in order to find one lost coin? Was there really a pearl merchant who sold his whole stock in order to buy one pearl which was

48

worth all the rest? Suppose that someone could prove beyond the shadow of a doubt that never, during the first century of the Christian era, did a Samaritan pay for the lodging of a Jew in an inn between Jerusalem and Jericho. What would this new evidence do to the parable of the Good Samaritan? Obviously, it would have no effect at all on the *truth* of the parable. The truth of this parable, and all the parables of Jesus, lies in the *meaning*, not in the factualness. The question is not whether it is fact or fiction, but rather what the story demands of us in the way of response.

The same principle holds true in the Old Testament. I am often asked, "Do you believe that the book of Jonah is true?" Why people so often single out this one book I'm not sure, but it seems to be a point of special concern. My answer to the question is "yes!" I do believe that the book of Jonah is true, but I do not believe that the truth of the book has much to do with the story of a fish. The problem with Jonah is that the fish has swallowed not only the prophet, but most of the meaning of the book!

The story about the fish is just a spectacular way of setting the stage for the real story of Jonah. When the Lord called Jonah as a prophet to Ninevah, Jonah did not want to go. Ninevah was the capital of Assyria, the most ruthless and bloodthirsty nation in the world.[3] Jonah was not surprised that God intended to destroy it, but he did not see any point in going there to warn the people to repent. The very idea of the Ninevites listening to his message was ridiculous. God might just as well get the destruction over with, and the sooner the better. Instead of going to Ninevah, Jonah started for Tarshish. God was not so easily denied, however, and Jonah ended up in Ninevah anyway. This, of course, is where the fish comes into the story.

Since he was forced to go there, Jonah did deliver to Ninevah the warning that God was about to destroy the city. However, he still considered the whole thing just a formality. He walked one third of the way across the city, telling the people to repent, and then went out to wait for the coming destruction. Forty days passed, and nothing happened. Jonah was puzzled. He went back into the city to see what the trouble was and could hardly believe his eyes. The Ninevites had heard his message and repented. Men, women, children, and even the farm animals were wearing sackcloth and ashes!

Any prophet should be delighted to see his work bear so much fruit. Not Jonah! Jonah was furious. He went out of the city and sat down on the ground to sulk. God was certainly losing his grip if he allowed a city like Ninevah to survive! God saw Jonah sulking and decided to teach him a lesson. The next day a plant sprang up next to Jonah and grew tall enough to shade him from the sun. Naturally, the prophet was delighted to have the shade. The next day the plant withered and died. Jonah was angry over the death of the plant.

"Do you miss that plant, Jonah?" asked the Lord.

"You know I do, Lord," Jonah replied.

"Are you sorry it died?"

"Of course I am!"

"Jonah, that was only a plant, and it was only here for one day; and yet you miss it, and you wish it had not died. Now, how do you suppose I would feel if I had to destroy a whole city full of my people? After all, the Ninevites are my people, too."

The truth of the book of Jonah is the love that God had for the people of Ninevah. Jonah thought God was wasting his time with them. What were they worth, anyway? His attitude was that of the Jews at the time of Ezra. The period of rebuilding Jerusalem after the return from Exile in Babylon was a time of intense nationalism. All foreigners were hated and feared. Ezra was insisting that Jews who had married foreign women had to deport them, along with their children. At this point, the story of Jonah was circulated to remind the Jews that God loved foreign nations as much as he loved his chosen people.[4]

Today, if we quibble over whether or not the "fish story" really happened, we miss the whole point of the book. The truth of the book is that God loves all nations equally, because they are all his children. In a day of iron and bamboo curtains, we need the book of Jonah to remind us that our enemies are God's children, whether they worship and serve him or not. It is much more comfortable, however, to ignore this issue and concentrate on the historicity of the story!

Another question I am often asked by laymen is whether or not I believe that the Bible contains *myth*. Actually, this question is as loaded and misleading as the question about fiction in the Bible. The word "myth" has several meanings. In common usage it can refer to something which is not true. For example, we say that a unicorn is a mythical animal because there are no unicorns, except in story books. Or we talk about the mythology of Greece and Rome, in which gods and goddesses of doubtful moral standards frolicked on Mount Olympus. Therefore, we have come to think of myth as something which is not real. Small wonder, then, that laymen are annoyed when scholars talk about the myths in the Bible. It sounds as though they are simply saying that the Bible is not true.

Such is not the case! The fact is that the *scholarly* definition of myth is not at all like the one referred to above. A biblical theologian defines myth as "an attempt to express the supernatural in natural terms, or the other-worldly in worldly terms." [5] In other words, myth would include any attempt to describe God or talk about God in human terms. Any such attempt is bound to be only partly successful. Human language is simply not capable of describing God.

For example, we call God our "heavenly Father." The word "Father" tells us something about God, but it is misleading. It says too much on the one hand, and too little on the other hand. My father is my mother's husband, but God is not. On the other hand, God has characteristics my father does not have. The word "Father" does not really describe God, but it gives us a *clue* as to *some* of the attributes of God. Thus, it is *mythological* to say that God is our father.

The word "heavenly" is also mythological. When we are asked where God is, we say he is "up in heaven." What does that really mean? When a Russian cosmonaut took a walk in space, he looked around to see if he could see God. When he came back, he reported that God was not up in heaven. Therefore, he concluded that God does not really exist. We laugh at his report and his conclusion, because we never really believed that God was in orbit around the world, anyway. But what do we mean, then, when we say that God is in heaven? The term had some meaning for first-century Christians because they knew where heaven was.[6] It was just beyond the hard blue dome which arched over the flat world on which they lived. They knew that this dome (called the firmament) had windows where the light of heaven could shine through at night. Since God did not live *on* the earth or *under* the earth, he must live up in heaven.

Today we know that this view of heaven and earth is scientifically wrong, but we still talk about God being up in heaven. The term "heaven" is mythological when it refers to God. The worst of it is that the myth has lost its meaning. It said something to the people who first used it, but it says little or nothing to us. In fact, it gets in our way when we try to talk about God to children who have seen moon shots on television. The Bible is filled with mythological statements about God which have lost some or all of their meaning as our understanding of the world has changed.

Either we have to give up speaking about God, or we have to reinterpret the biblical statements about him in terms which are meaningful today. Obviously, we can't do the former. The latter is called *demythologizing* the Bible.[7] Some people panic when they hear the word "demythologizing." They are afraid that it means cutting the heart out of the Bible. On the contrary, it really means trying to put the meaning of the Bible into language which is meaningful for today. This is a complicated process which we cannot take time to discuss in detail here. It tries to distinguish between the message or meaning of the Bible and the language in which this message is presented.

Certainly our concern, as Christians, is in the message, not the language. Translating the Greek and Hebrew of the Bible into English—even modern English—does not get rid of the language problem. We are still left with words like "heaven" which do not mean much to a twentieth-century man. If the Bible is to be believed in a scientific age, we have to determine the meaning behind the first-century terms and concepts and present that meaning in terms which not only make sense to modern man, but force him into a confrontation with the living Christ today. Therefore, the question of meaning in the Bible is much more important than questions about fiction or myth in its pages. This means that we must take a look at our "scientific" way of thinking and speaking today, to see how it relates to the meaning of the Bible.

4 Science and/or Religion

Modern man cannot read the Bible without confronting the problem of religion and science. We live in a scientific age. To a great degree, our conception of reality is determined by scientific method. Yet in religion, and particularly in the Bible, we seem to find ourselves in a different world, where science has little or no meaning. The dilemma of today's Christian is how to live in both worlds at the same time.

In order to shed light on this problem and perhaps point to a solution, it might be well to compare science and theology as disciplines. To begin with, we can see that they are separated by a basic difference in method.

Science uses *inductive* reasoning, while theology is *deductive*.[1]

These terms may sound difficult, but the ideas behind them are really quite simple. In the *inductive* method of seeking knowledge, the researcher begins by observing many individual events or objects. On the basis of these observations, he begins to see some sort of pattern. He tries to explain the pattern with a theory, called a "hypothesis." Then he works out an experiment to test his theory. Usually, his experiment shows that the theory is only partly right. It explains part of the pattern, but not all of it. So he modifies his theory a bit and tests it again in another experiment. After many experiments and modified theories he comes up with a hypothesis which seems satisfactory. Other scientists then test this hypothesis with the same or similar experiments. If their findings agree with his, then they also accept his theory. Now the theory is called a "scientific fact." On the basis of this fact, scientists are able to predict what will happen in certain situations. What the scientist has done, then, is to draw a general conclusion from specific bits of information. Inductive reasoning always goes from the *specific* to the *general*.

Let's take a look at a very simple example of this process at work. Suppose that our scientist is looking at crows. He goes out and observes several dozen of these birds and notices that all of them are black. He therefore proposes the theory that *all* crows are black. Then he tests his theory. He observes several thousand

57

crows and asks other observers about the crows they have seen. When the evidence is in, he discovers that out of some ten thousand crows observed, all but two were black. Those two were white. On further investigation he discovers that those two were albino crows, with no coloring at all in their feathers. His revised hypothesis, then, is that all crows are black unless they are albino. This is accepted as a scientific fact until proved otherwise. It is a general statement, drawn from observations of specific individual crows. The generalization is drawn on the basis of a sample, rather than on the basis of a knowledge of *all* crows. The scientist trusts that what is true of a reasonable sample of the crow population will be true of the whole group.

The *deductive* reasoning used by theology, on the other hand, is quite different. While inductive reasoning goes from the specific to the general, deductive reasoning goes from the general to the specific. The theologian *begins* with a general statement. For example, he may say, "God loves all men." Then he applies this general principle to specific situations. If God loves all men, then he loves each individual man, including you and me. Another general principle might be, If God loves us we ought to love one another. This means that I should love you, and that you should love me. You can see how this form of reasoning goes from the general to the specific. Thus the methods of reasoning used by the theologian and the scientist are precisely opposite.

This difference in method leads to a second difference between science and religion. Science starts from a position of skepticism, while theology starts from a position of belief. The scientist doubts everything, including his own theories, until proof has been provided through experimentation. When a theory proves to be correct, the scientist accepts it tentatively until new evidence is available.

The theologian, on the other hand, begins with a statement of faith. When the scientist asks him where his faith statement came from, he says that it is revelation from God. But this is not a category which the scientist can handle, according to his methods. His approach to any statement is to devise an experiment by which it can be proved or disproved. No such experiment can be found to deal with the statement "God is love." Since the statement cannot be proved experimentally, the scientist cannot accept it as a fact. On the other hand, he cannot devise an experiment to disprove it. His only response to such a statement, as a scientist, can be to lay it aside and say, "I don't know." This is called an agnostic position, from the Latin word *agnosco,* meaning "I don't know."

Since science and theology use opposite methods of reasoning, and since one begins with skepticism while the other begins with faith, it is difficult for the scientist and the theologian to communicate or even to understand each other. Therefore, they have tended to go their own ways, each thinking that his field has little need for the other. Through the centuries, the theologian has felt secure in believing that his discipline provided satisfactory answers to all life's important questions. Now, some scientists have reached the same conclusion about science. The belief that science provides sufficient answers to all important questions may be called "scientism." It is important enough to our discussion of religion and science that we should take time to analyze it.

The scientific achievements of the past fifty years have been remarkable. Scientific method has provided us with a staggering amount of knowledge. We now know as much about outer space as we used to know about our own planet just a short time ago. Science has probed into the depths of the sea to unlock its secrets. The atom, once thought to be the smallest particle of matter, can now be divided into its component parts so that each can be studied individually. Diseases which once killed people by the thousands have now been virtually wiped out. Science has probed into the recesses of the human mind to discover a great deal about the basis of our behavior. Computers now do in minutes jobs which would take men days or weeks to complete by themselves. Scientific farming can increase crop yields many times over. Atomic power can be used to run most of the world's industry—or to wipe out human life entirely. It is no wonder that modern man has developed a healthy respect for science and what it can do.

Before science was developed, men believed that all of life was in the hands of supernatural powers. When disease strikes in a primitive society, a witch doctor is called in to drive out the evil spirit which caused the illness. Science has replaced the witch doctor with a physician, a hospital, a medical laboratory, and wonder drugs. When a primitive society suffers a crop failure, sacrifices are made to the gods of fertility so that they will send a better harvest the following year. Science has replaced the fertility gods with fertilizer, insecticides, and hybrid seed.

Many things once in the realm of religion are now in the realm of science instead. Because of this, scientism contends that religion lives only in the "gaps" of science. As science develops, so the theory goes, the area of life to which religion applies keeps shrinking. Eventually, scientists will know enough about all natural events and human behavior so that religion will not be needed at all. Therefore, religion can be tolerated only as a sort of stopgap to keep people happy until science comes up with the *real* answers to their problems.

This proposition sounds plausible at first hearing, but under close scrutiny it turns out to have some flaws. The fact is that science is not closing the knowledge gap between what we know and what we want to know, but is actually widening it. The solving of a scientific problem often opens up several new problems. The use of wonder drugs in fighting bacteria has produced a race of bacteria which thrive on the drugs which killed their ancestors. Some of the failures of science are as spectacular as its achievements. Medical science is no closer to a cure for the common cold than it was fifty years ago. Furthermore, many of the greatest problems facing society today are products of the scientific revolution. A good case in point is the threat of thermonuclear war now hanging over the world. We now have the technology to wipe out starvation in the world, or to wipe out the human race. Which it will be is a question that lies more within the area of religion than of science.

One further observation on the sufficiency—either actual or potential—of science: such a belief is a matter of faith, not of proof. Since there is no way to prove or disprove it, the true scientist must be an agnostic on the question of scientism. If he insists that science has a sufficient answer to all important questions, he is operating like a theologian, not like a scientist.

A corollary of scientism which is quite popular today is the idea that scientific truth is somehow more accurate or more true than religious truth. After all, scientific statements deal with things you can see or touch or hear. Science deals with the world as it *is*. If one scientist does an experiment and publishes his work, any other scientist can do the same experiment and come out with the same results. Certainly, then, scientific truth must be of a different order than theological statements which deal with things no one can see or test.

It is dificult to test the relative truthfulness of scientific and religious statements, but we *can* test the hypothesis that scientific truth is absolute truth. Any good scientist will tell you that all his statements are only *approximations* of the truth. Read any current scientific textbook in nearly any field of science, and compare it with a similar textbook published ten or fifteen years ago. Things which were "true" ten years ago are "false" today. How many of the things which are true today will be false five years from now?

The further you go in science, the more scientific and theological statements seem to have in common. For decades scientists debated the issue of the nature of light. Is it made up of waves or particles? Today, the generally accepted answer to this question is "yes." How can it be *both* waves and particles? Physicists don't know the answer to that question any more than you do. Under some conditions the answer comes out one way, under other conditions it comes out the other. Physicists have now decided simply to accept this paradox or contradiction and work with it.

There was a time, not long ago, when scientists thought paradoxes were the exclusive property of theologians. However, many scientific concepts have changed rather dramatically since Einstein introduced his theories of relativity. Even on a fairly basic level, science finds itself depending on concepts which are hard to pin down. Nothing that I learned in theological school was more unreal or hard to understand than the theory of imaginary numbers taught in my high school algebra class. After explaining that the square root of —1 was a logical impossibility, the teacher announced that we were going to pretend that it existed anyway, and use it. We did, and it made a whole area of mathematics much easier to work with. Higher mathematics is full of such paradoxes, and mathematics is the language of science!

Now let's try to sum up what we have said about science. It has an impressive list of accomplishments to its credit. However, it cannot prove its own sufficiency as a source of truth. Furthermore, all scientific truth is approximate rather than absolute. Therefore, we can neither ignore the importance of science, nor accept the claims of scientism. Science and theology are not enemies. In fact, they seem to have much in common in spite of their differences. However, a scientism which denies the importance of religion is nonscientific in its method.

Let us now turn from our examination of science to the question of how the Bible should be read in a scientific age. On the surface, it might appear that the Bible and science are incompatible. For example, scientific accounts of the beginning of the world do not agree with the first two chapters of Genesis. The miracle stories of both the Old and New Testaments are difficult to explain or understand scientifically. In scientific terms the resurrection of Christ from the dead is nearly incredible, and his ascension into heaven is absurd.

Today's Christian cannot simply ignore such scientific

judgments, nor fail to take them seriously. How, then, can he take the Bible seriously? One of the easiest ways would be to develop a split-level mind. In dealing with today's world, you would accept scientific method and think in scientific terms. In dealing with the Bible, you would make a mental shift into another world. You would believe that the sun revolves around the earth. You would believe that the world was created in six days of twenty-four hours each. You would believe that the earth is flat, heaven is just beyond the blue of the sky, and stars are the windows of heaven through which angels come and go. The Bible, for you, would exist in one world and daily life in another. Nothing in our "scientific" world could affect your faith in the Bible or any part of it.

One problem with this approach is that it cuts both ways. It might save your faith in the literal accuracy of the Bible, but you would pay a high price for its doing so. For if today's world cannot affect your faith in the Bible, then your faith in the Bible has nothing to say to your daily life. Thus the Bible, though preserved intact, would be rendered useless as a guide for your life. It would be meaningful in church on Sunday morning, but not at the office on Tuesday afternoon. To a split-level mind the Bible is as irrelevant as it is correct!

Another approach to the problem posed by science and the Bible is to say that the Bible is really scientifically accurate. Any conflicts between science and religion are explained away as a misunderstanding of what the biblical text really means. Some Christian scientists have labored long and hard to prove this hypothesis. They point out that many of the passages in the Bible are amazingly accurate when read scientifically. For example, the present nation of Israel has used the Old Testament to determine where wheat should be grown and where oil might be found. Many of the healing miracles in the Bible can now be explained in terms of our knowledge of psychosomatic medicine. Astronomers can now explain the appearance of the Star of Bethlehem by a calculation of the positions of several bright planets at about the time Jesus was born.

On the basis of this sort of information, it can be suggested that every verse in the Bible is scientifically accurate, if read correctly. Thus, "Every valley shall be lifted up and every mountain and hill be made low" (Isaiah 40:4) would refer to erosion of mountains and the deposit of silt in valleys. Similarly, "All flesh is grass," two verses later, means that all animals eat grasses or feed on animals that do. This reading of the latter passage ignores the fact that the reference to grass, in context, was obviously meant by the author as a metaphor rather than a literal statement.

To read Isaiah 40 in this way suggests that the author was not really speaking to his own people at all. He was really a crypto-scientist who was writing his message for the twentieth century. To the prescientific Hebrew, the whole thing was in a code which he was not supposed to understand. The *real* message was just to lie there unheard until the dawn of *our* age, and the whole Bible was really written just for our generation. The nicest name we could give to this attitude is "massive arrogance."

If we turn to the book of Genesis, we see that this approach to reading the Bible simply will not stand up. For example, look at the order of creation in Genesis 1. Light is created and shines on the earth in verse 3. Plants are created in verse 12. But the sun, which is the source of the earth's light and without which plants cannot exist, is not created until verse 16. What kind of scientific accuracy is this? Furthermore, there are two different creation stories in Genesis, and they are quite different. In Genesis 2:3 the process of creation is complete. In 2:4 it begins all over again. Man is created in 1:26. He is created a second time in 2:7. If you are going to read the book of Genesis as a book of science, you are inclined to reject the first creation story and accept the second. But why should Genesis be read scientifically? It is intended to be a book of theology, not a book of science.

If you read Genesis as science you have to choose one of the creation stories as accurate and reject the other. If you read it as theology you can accept both. The editor who put these two stories together in Genesis 1 and 2 was either an idiot, or he did not think that the stories contradicted each other. And if he read them as saying the same thing, he was reading them theologically. He understood them as saying something about God and about the world as his creation.

Let me illustrate this approach to the problem of science and the Bible by sharing a personal experience. Several years ago a high school student from my church came into my study, obviously much disturbed. His problem, he said, was that he wanted to become a research scientist. Thinking that his problem was a financial one, because his parents did not have the means to send him to college, I reassured him about the availability of scholarships. But this was not his concern.

"I want to be a research scientist, but I also want to be a Christian," he said. "I don't see how the two can go together. The things I read in science textbooks in high school don't seem to fit with the things I read in the Bible. Science and the Bible have different stories of how man was created. They have different ideas about how the world began. I don't see how I can work as a scientist and believe in the Bible. When the two contradict each other, which one am I supposed to believe?"

As I thought for a moment about an answer to John's question, I reached back to the shelf behind me and pulled out a book. "What science course are you going to take in the fall?" I asked.

"Next year I have chemistry," he replied.

"In your chemistry class next year, I'd like to have you try something for me."

John looked at me quizzically, not quite sure what

I was getting at. "What do you want me to do?" he asked.

"I would like to have you use this book as your chemistry textbook." As I handed the book to him, he looked at me as though I had suddenly grown a second head.

"How can I use this as a chemistry textbook?" he asked in amazement. "This isn't a chemistry book, it's just a dictionary."

"I know what it is," I replied. "But give me one good reason why you can't use it as a science textbook."

"That's a crazy idea." John replied. "A dictionary doesn't have any chemistry in it!"

"Well, let's see whether there's any chemistry here or not," I suggested. We picked a page at random and found there two definitions of chemical terms. Then we turned to another page and discovered another definition which applied to chemistry. The third page to which we turned at random even had a chart of the elements according to their atomic weights. We tried ten or a dozen pages, and each one had at least one chemical definition.

"Well, we apparently don't have a problem," I suggested. "This dictionary is just full of chemistry, so obviously you can use it for a chemistry textbook, can't you?"

"No, I can't, and you know it! The dictionary may have a lot of chemistry in it but it wasn't written to be a textbook. It was written to be a dictionary." John

69

caught my smile and suddenly realized what I had been driving at all along. "I think I see what you mean," he said. "You have to use every book for the purpose for which it was written, is that it?"

"Right you are! The chemistry book and the dictionary may contain the same material, but it was put together in different ways according to the purposes of the authors. If you try to use a dictionary as a textbook, you'll be in trouble. On the other hand, if you try to use a chemistry textbook as a dictionary, you won't come out any better. In order to take chemistry next year, you will have to have one of each, won't you?"

Again John was puzzled. "Why will I need a dictionary?" he asked.

"How will you know the meanings of all the new chemical terms without a dictionary?"

"Oh, that's easy. There's a glossary in the back of . . . Oh! A glossary is really a dictionary, isn't it?"

"Right!" I smiled. "You have to have both a dictionary and a textbook to get the full picture of chemistry, and you have to use each one for the purpose for which it was written. Now, where does this discussion lead us in terms of the Bible and science?"

"I see what you are driving at," John replied. "You are saying that a scientific textbook tells the story from one perspective and the Bible tells it from another, is that it?"

"Exactly, John. The Bible may look like a science textbook because it deals with some of the problems of science, like the origin of man. But similar subject matter doesn't make a dictionary a chemistry text nor the Bible a science text. You must read each book on its own terms, in the light of its purpose."

John began with the false assumption that religion and science are in conflict because they take different approaches. The conflict is not between theology and science but between those who misunderstand the purpose of one or both.

Each discipline gives us valuable insights into the way things are, from its own perspective. These insights are not identical, but they complement each other. We might describe their relationship with a modern parable. Imagine two men standing by the seashore, admiring the beauty of surf crashing on huge rocks. For a long time each man stands spellbound. Then each goes his own way. One returns to his canvas and brushes, to recapture the beauty of the scene in oil colors. The other re-creates the seashore scene in words as he writes a poem. The oil painting and the poem are as different as a Bible and a geology textbook. Yet each is a reflection of the same scene, according to one man's perspective.

Science, from its perspective, has widened our knowledge of the universe considerably. Theology deals with problems of *meaning,* to which science, by definition, has no answers. Today we need both disciplines in order to live. Theology which ignores the importance of science is meaningless for the twentieth century. Science

71

which avoids the ethical and moral questions of theology threatens the peace of the world and the whole future of mankind.

Science and theology can and must complement each other. However, it is easier to accept this idea on the abstract level than it is to apply it to specific situations—for example, to the question of biblical miracles.

5 What About Miracles?

How should modern man read the miracle stories in the Bible today? For those who take the Bible seriously, this is one of the most difficult questions to answer.

Some people say that miracles should just be ignored. After all, they don't fit in with the way we understand things today. Twentieth-century men understand and discuss things scientifically. Everything that happens has a logical explanation, doesn't it? We know that water doesn't turn into wine. We know that men don't walk on water. If the Bible says that these things did happen, shouldn't we just treat the Bible like a fairy tale or science fiction?

Obviously this sort of answer won't do at all! The Bible is far too important to be dismissed just because it contains miracle stories. Some devoted Christians would go much further than this. The Bible is important, they say, precisely *because* it contains miracle stories. Perhaps these stories were put in the Bible in order to test our faith today. Anyone can believe things that he sees with his own eyes. The real test of faith is to believe things which cannot be proved. Isn't this what the author of Hebrews is saying when he calls faith "the substance of things hoped for, the evidence of things not seen"? (Hebrews 11:1 KJV.)

This attitude toward biblical miracles is a bit like a scene in Lewis Carroll's book *Through the Looking Glass,* in which the White Queen asks Alice to believe something impossible. Alice just laughs. "There's no use trying," she says, "one *can't* believe impossible things."

"I dare say you haven't had much practice," says the Queen. "When I was your age, I always did it for half an hour a day. Why, sometimes I've believed as many as six impossible things before breakfast!"

We smile at the idea of the White Queen believing six impossible things before breakfast, but we have to take seriously the point Mr. Carroll was making. One theologian several centuries ago said that he *enjoyed* finding absurd and incredible things in the Bible. The more absurd they seemed to him, the prouder he felt when he believed them.[1] But does the God who gave us the power of reason enjoy seeing us lay this reason aside when we pick up the Bible? If we can't believe the Bible in the same way we believe anything else, then how can our belief in the Bible make a difference in the way we live in the everyday world?

If we can neither ignore miracle stories nor accept them as fact simply because they are in the Bible, then how *can* we deal with them? Perhaps the best way would be to try to explain them in scientific terms, by guessing what *really* might have happened.

This method of interpretation is often used with a story like the feeding of the five thousand (John 6:1-13). It is suggested that the people who went out into the wilderness with Jesus really had food with them all the time. After all, no one would be silly enough to go so far from home without taking some food. Probably, each person had his lunch hidden under his long, flowing robe. When the dinner hour arrived, no one dared show the food he had brought, for fear it would be stolen by the hungry crowd. When Jesus realized what was happening he decided to teach the people a lesson. He called a small boy to him and asked him what he had brought to eat. The boy showed him a few pieces of unleavened bread and dried fish. Jesus asked him to share his food with the crowd. The boy agreed. When Jesus began to hand out tiny pieces of bread and fish, the adults in the crowd were ashamed of their selfishness. Sheepishly they brought out their own food and began to share it with one another. When everyone had eaten there was still some food left over.

This is an ingenious explanation, but it leaves a number of questions unanswered. Why do the Gospels have stories of feeding four thousand people and then five thousand people? [2] If the story only means that the people *shared* their food, why doesn't it say so? What does the story really *mean?* Why was it remembered? Why was it recorded in the Gospels? What is its importance for us today? Can we expect Jesus to feed us in the same way? Furthermore, how can we apply this method of interpretation to other stories, such as the raising of Lazarus after he had been dead for several days? It appears that neither this approach nor any of the other approaches we have discussed so far is really a satisfactory way to look at miracles.

Perhaps the problem is that we are looking at these miracle stories in the wrong way. Maybe the whole problem is a lot simpler than it seems. The fact is that according to our definitions *there are no miracle stories in the Bible!* This sounds preposterous! Isn't the story of the opening of the Red Sea in the Old Testament? Doesn't the New Testament tell of Jesus' walking on the water and raising Lazarus from the dead and turning water into wine? Of course! Well, aren't these miracle stories? No, not according to the standard definition of a miracle.

According to the dictionary, there are two factors which make up a miracle. In the first place, a miracle is something which is a violation of natural law. It cannot be explained in terms of the known laws of physics, chemistry, and biology. In the second place, because a miracle is a violation of natural law, it is thought to be an act of God.

On this basis we look at the Red Sea story as a miracle. In the first place, no natural laws can explain the opening of the Red Sea. Since we can't explain this, then naturally we say that it was an act of God. On the same basis we call the raising of Lazarus from the dead and Jesus' walking on the water, "miracles."

Suppose, though, we were able to sit down with the author of the book of Exodus or one of the Gospels. If we were to discuss natural law with an Old or New Testament author, all we would get is a blank look. The Hebrews and the early Christians had no concept of natural law. They knew that certain things happened more often than other things, but they had no knowledge of physics, chemistry, or biology. Since they knew nothing about natural law, they did not think of events as violating laws.

In the second place, the biblical authors would be offended by the idea that only *some* events were acts of God. As far as they were concerned, *every* event was an act of God. When the sun rose in the morning, in the biblical view, it was because God had made it rise. When the Hebrews escaped from Egypt, it was an act of God. When the Babylonians captured Jerusalem and took the Jews into exile, this was another act of God. When King Cyrus of Persia captured Babylon and sent the Jews home again, this too was seen as an act of God.

Since natural laws were unknown in the biblical period and since everything was thought to be an act of God, the idea of "miracle" as we know it was completely foreign to the biblical writers. As far as they were concerned, the Exile and the Exodus were exactly the same kind of event. In each case God was acting in history in order to show his will to his people.

The idea of miracles is a modern idea. No one would think of talking about the airplanes in the Bible, since the airplane is a modern invention that was not known in biblical times. Perhaps the idea of miracles is nearly as modern as the idea of airplanes, and therefore we cannot talk meaningfully about miracles in the Bible.

But isn't this too easy an explanation? Aren't there events in the Bible which appear miraculous to us? Of course there are. Isn't the word "miracle" found in the Bible itself? Yes, in most of our English translations it is there. However, the Hebrew and Greek words which we translate as "miracle" do not mean what we mean by this word.

If what we call miracles in the Bible are not really miracles, then what are they? In biblical terms they are "signs." If the importance of a miracle is its *miraculousness,* then the importance of a sign is its *significance.* You may never have noticed before that the word "significance" begins with the word "sign." "Significance" means "the importance of a sign."

We sometimes say that miracles are important because they prove the existence or power of God. Actually, no

Old or New Testament author questioned the existence or power of God. Therefore, a miracle would have had no meaning for him. Signs, on the other hand, reveal the purpose of God and his will for men.

When we read a story such as the Exodus or the walking on the water or the raising of Lazarus, we cannot make sense out of it unless we ask the right questions.[3] It makes little sense to ask, How does this story prove God? The biblical writer did not use it to prove God. It does no good to ask, What really did happen? Those who witnessed the event and preserved the story were not interested in a scientific or historical explanation of what "really happened." They were interested only in what the story meant as a sign. Therefore, our question has to be, What does the story mean? We have to try to put ourselves back into the situation of the biblical authors. The story of the Exodus appears to mean that God was the protector and ruler of his people. The story of the feeding of the crowd said that Jesus Christ was the Bread of Life (see John 6:30-35). The raising of Lazarus meant that Christ is the Resurrection and the Life (John 11:25).

Since we are modern men, we naturally want to ask modern questions. When we deal with a first-century story, however, we have to settle for first-century questions. A man's mental set always determines what he sees and hears. If you wish, you can prove this to yourself with an interesting little game.

Gather two or three other people and tell them to

concentrate closely on what you say. Ask each of them to imagine that he is the operator of an elevator. Then take the elevator on an imaginary trip. The trip begins with, let us say, four people on the elevator. For each stop, tell your friends how many people get on the elevator and how many get off. As you take the elevator on its imaginary trip, be sure that you keep track of the number of stops it makes. After six or seven stops, ask the people who have been listening to you, "How many stops did the elevator make?" Unless they have played the game before, the only answer you will get is some blank stares. You will discover that everyone has been counting people instead of stops. Those who heard the story won't be able to tell how many stops the elevator made. On the other hand, *you* probably won't know how many people were left on the elevator at the last stop.

Whomever you try this game on becomes the victim of his own presuppositions. When he hears you tell him about the number of people on the elevator, he jumps to the conclusion that this is a game of counting *people*. Because he has been concentrating on the wrong factor (from your point of view), he cannot answer your question. Even though he heard all you said, his point of view has robbed him of the ability to deal with that question.

Now let's go back to our Bible stories for a second look. The Gospel writers have given us several unusual stories about Jesus. Those who saw the event and wrote

80

the story knew nothing about science or natural law. They were not the least bit interested in the "how" of what happened. They were interested in the *meaning* of the event. Telling the story exactly as it happened was not important as long as the meaning was not changed. If changing or rearranging the details of the story made the meaning stand out more clearly, then the changes were made. Furthermore, many of the details were simply ignored because of the author's concentration on meaning.

Now the story comes to my attention. As a modern man I read it with certain presuppositions. For one thing, I have a scientific world view. I know about natural laws, and I'm suspicious of things which seem to contradict them. Therefore, I ask the question, What really happened? I want the kind of answer that a newspaper reporter would have given if he had been there. I want the facts that would satisfy a scientist. But these answers and facts are not available. All I can find out is what the author chose to record *from his point of view.*

If I ask the same questions that the biblical author asked, I can get meainingful answers. If I ask modern questions, I don't get any answers. It's the elevator game all over again. The only way you can win is to start out with the same point of view as the one telling the story. The question, What really happened? is as meaningless as the question, How high is up? Since we cannot make twentieth-century men out of biblical authors, we have to give up twentieth-century questions about biblical stories. Whether we like it or not, we shall never know what really happened in any of the miracle stories. The stories are statements of faith about theological meanings. There is no way that we can reconstruct modern "explanations" from them.

Often, the meaning of a story is found in a single statement by Jesus at the conclusion of the story. "I am the bread of life," "I am the resurrection and the life," "O man of little faith, why did you doubt?" (Matthew 14:31.)

We may be annoyed at having to settle for meanings rather than explanations, but there is nothing we can do about it. The miracles can never be reconstructed. Behind each miracle story is an unusual event which actually happened. People remembered the event, and they remembered what Jesus said when the event took place. The quotation and the meaning of the event were remembered. The details were ignored and forgotten. When the story was retold, details were supplied as needed. They were not important as long as they pointed to the correct meaning of the story.

The situation might be compared to a story I heard recently. Johnny had been studying the story of the Exodus in his second grade Sunday school class, and his mother asked him to tell her the story. "Well," said Johnny, "Moses and his men were trying to get away from Pharaoh's army. When they got to the Red Sea, they looked back, and there came Pharaoh's jeeps and tanks after them. Moses called for his engineers, and in no time at all they threw a pontoon bridge across the sea. The Hebrews got across all right, and then Pharaoh's men started across after them. Moses called for a demolition crew to blow up the bridge. The demolition crew came in and blew it to pieces, so that Pharaoh and all his men were drowned, and that's how God saved his people from Pharaoh."

"Johnny," said his mother, "is that really the way the teacher told the story?"

"Well, not quite," Johnny answered, "but if I told it the way she did, you'd *never* believe me!"

The story is humorous, but it makes a vital point. Johnny saw that the importance of the story was its meaning. He kept the meaning intact, even though he changed the details. Since the details weren't really important, he didn't mind changing them.

The main point of this discussion of miracles is that understanding their meaning is more important than "believing" them in the ordinary sense. Sometimes people try to impress us with their Christian faith by testifying to their faith in the Bible. "I believe the Virgin Birth story!" they will say. "I believe that Jesus walked on the water! I believe that he changed water into wine! I believe that he raised Lazarus from the dead!"

My reply to this testimony is, "Fine! I'm glad you believe these stories. More power to you! Now, what *difference* in your life has your belief in these stories made *this week?*"

Believing that something is true is not nearly as important as doing something about its meaning. A couple of years ago, I read a manual on flying. When I finished the book I knew how to fly an airplane. Furthermore, I believed every word in the book. I was convinced that everything in the book was true. Did that make me a pilot? Of course not. I can never be a pilot until I go out and *practice* the principles in the book.

So it is with the Bible. Believing that the miracle stories are literally true isn't very important. Doing something about the *meaning* of the stories is!

6 History
Then and Now

In our last chapter, we discussed miracles as one of the biblical stumbling blocks for modern man. We tried to suggest that the miracle stories be read for their meaning rather than for their literal sense as we see it. Let us now look at some other problem areas of modern Bible readers. A good place to begin is the rather confusing problem of biblical history.

What is history? That sounds like a foolish question, doesn't it? Isn't history simply a record of what has happened in the past? Webster's dictionary defines it as a "systematic written account of events, particularly of those affecting a nation, institution, science, or art."

It may be that this definition is too simple. If history is just a "systematic written account of events" then why don't all histories of the same period agree? Canadian and American textbooks disagree on who really won the War of 1812. Russian and American textbooks disagree on the events of World War II, and particularly on what has happened in the Cold War. Even in United States history, the writing depends partly on the political, social, and regional background of the author.[1]

It is sometimes difficult to match up the truth of an event with what is reported about it. Not long ago I happened on the scene of a two-car collision. No one was hurt, but both cars were badly damaged. Beside the drivers stood a policeman with a notebook. Each man was waving his arms and shouting to get the policeman's attention. I rolled down the car window and listened for a few moments to what they were saying. According to the two stories, these men seemed to have been in two different accidents. Their stories didn't agree at all. Each man claimed that he was right and the other was a liar. The policeman obviously didn't know whom to believe. Finally, he wrote down both stories and left the decision as to what really happened to the insurance companies.

There is no such thing as completely "pure" or "objective" history. Any written account of what has happened in the past is bound to be the author's *interpretation* of the events. Although he may try to be honest and objective, there is no way that he can avoid putting something of himself into the history. There are at least two points at which a historian puts the stamp of his personality on the history that he writes. The first is in his selection of material. No one, in writing history, can include everything that happened. The historian has to select the events he considers to be most important and most meaningful. No matter how the selection is made, it slants and colors the history. In the second place, the author has to arrange his material after he has selected it. Both the selection and the arrangement reflect the author's own points of view and his cultural background.

It is interesting to look through various books of history to see how authors have selected the material and arranged it. On the basis of the material they select, writers can be divided up into categories or "schools" of history.

Some historians fall into the *great man* school. They think that history can best be told by writing biography. They see events as determined by the decisions of outstanding leaders. Thus, World War II would be seen as a result of the personality and the dreams of Adolf Hitler. The New Deal Administration in the 30's and 40's in our country would be credited mainly to the mind of Franklin Roosevelt.

On the other hand, some historians think that everything depends on *cultural and political movements.* From this point of view, Hitler's Germany was the result of frustrations coming out of the World War

I Treaty of Versailles, which put Germany at a great disadvantage among her European neighbors. The New Deal, in turn, would be seen as a response to the depression following the stock market crash of 1929.

Some historians see history as being primarily *political*. When they write, they arrange their material around major political events, such as changes in national leadership. Other authors feel that the history of the world is the history of its *military exploits*. Their history books gave a picture of the rise and fall of military powers and the importance of the crucial battles that changed the course of history. Still other historians feel that the key to history lies not in great men, whether politicians or military leaders, but in the *development of technology*. They feel that the turning points of history are such things as the invention of the wheel, the industrial revolution, and the development of atomic power. No matter what an author's particular philosophy of history is, it is easy to see that this philosophy determines the events which he selects as the crucial points of history.

Once the material has been selected, it has to be arranged. The history which results depends on how the arranging is done. This point may be more difficult to accept than the idea that selection is important. What valid arrangement of events can there be other than chronological order? The only way that history makes any sense, as far as we are concerned, is when it follows the order in which the events themselves took place.

Imagine a man trying to write the story of his day like this:

"I arrived at the office and found that I had more work than I expected. On the way home from the office my car stopped and I had to spend two hours getting it repaired, so I was late to dinner. I went to lunch and was pleasantly surprised to land a new contract. When I sat down at the breakfast table my wife told me that the car had been sounding funny, but I told her that she didn't know anything about automobiles. When I got home from the office I found that the neighbor's dog had chewed up our newspaper, which didn't help my frame of mind. On the way to the office, I didn't hear any strange noises in the car, so I knew that my wife was wrong again. I asked my boss why he had given me these two extra jobs, and he told me there was no one else intelligent enough to handle them; that helped a little bit. Finally, when I sat down to watch television the tube blew out and that was just the last straw. As soon as I got up this morning, I broke a shoe lace in trying to tie my shoes and I knew I was going to have a bad day."

The sentences in this "history of a hard day" could be arranged to make good sense. The way they are arranged now, they make very strange history indeed. We say it is strange because we know that history has to be written chronologically. The point is so obvious that it never occurs to us to question it. How could anybody write meaningful history any other way? The fact is that writing history in chronological order is simply an *accepted convention of our culture.* History written any other way looks strange to us. We would rather ignore it or sneer at it than question our presupposition.

Another convention that we follow in reading and writing history is that the story must answer the questions "who, where, what, when, why, and how." It is no coincidence that these are the questions that a newspaper reporter is taught to ask when he goes out to cover a story. When we read history we want to know "facts." We take it for granted that the meaning of an event is found by asking the newspaper reporter's questions. This makes it difficult for us to read history written by someone with a different point of view. For example, suppose that a writer believes that the importance or meaning of history is found in discovering *God's action* in it. This sort of history would be difficult for us to understand. If newspaper reporters started writing all their stories in terms of what God is doing in the situation, we would probably start buying another newspaper. That approach simply wouldn't be appropriate for the situation. On the other hand, we seem to find nothing strange in taking our "newspaper reporter" understanding of history into the Bible, and reading the Bible as though it were the morning paper.

Twentieth-century man must read the Bible in the terms in which it was written. We must remember that Old Testament authors often paid little attention to the order of events. It was understood that God had an

overarching purpose for history. All events took place
as God caused them to happen. However, in the eyes of
God time was not very important. As the Psalmist said,
for God there is no difference between a day and a
thousand years (Psalm 90:4). The important question
for Hebrew history was, What is God's plan and purpose for us? rather than, In what order did events of the
past take place?

We have already seen in Chapter 4 that there are two
different stories of the creation.[2] In I Samuel 31 and
II Samuel 1, there are two different accounts of the
death of King Saul and his sons. At the end of the book
of Joshua, the conquest of Canaan had been completed.
The Canaanites and all the other people who had lived
there before the Hebrews arrived had been driven out.
However, in the first chapter of the book of Judges
(which immediately follows Joshua) it appears that
the conquest is not yet finished. The whole first chapter
of Judges deals with the driving out of the original
inhabitants of the land. In the books of Samuel and
Kings we have the story of Israel and Judah from the
time of Saul, who died about 1000 B.C., to the Babylonian exile of the Hebrews, about 585 B.C. Then the
story is told again in the books of I and II Chronicles,
in a somewhat different way.

Obviously, the Hebrew writers and editors could have
smoothed out this history into one well organized narrative, but they chose not to do so. No one today would
pay much attention to a history book which jumped

and skipped around as much as the Old Testament does. When scholars write Old Testament history today, they must spend long weary hours trying to sort out the events and put them into the order which they probably happened.

The Hebrews were simply not as much concerned about time sequence as we are. We can see this quite clearly when we take a look at the Hebrew language itself. In English all our verbs have tenses. A verb in the present tense, such as "I walk, means that the action is going on right now. If the verb is in the past tense, such as "I walked," we know that the action took place in the past. "I shall walk" indicates the future, showing that the action has not yet taken place. The English language has several other tenses including the perfect, pluperfect, and future perfect, to show other time relationships in terms of the action described. The most amazing thing about the Hebrew language, for beginning students, is the fact that the verbs have no tenses at all. In biblical Hebrew, there is no way to express the difference between "I am going" and "I shall go." Hebrew has no past, present, or future.

A Hebrew verb is either in the completed form or the incomplete form.[3] If the verb is in the completed form the action has already been finished. A verb in the incomplete form means that the action has not been finished. But there is no way to determine whether or not the action has already started. For many verbs, the participle form is used. This simply means that action is going on, with no reference at all to time or to completion. Not only does all this lead to a different attitude toward time on the part of the Hebrews, but it raises some interesting questions of Bible translation.

A scholar who translates the Hebrew Bible into English has to provide tenses for all the Hebrew verbs. This means he has to decide whether the author would have wanted a verb to be past, present, or future. No matter what decision he makes, the scholar is reading his own interpretation into the English translation whenever he choses a tense. Imagine the difficulty that results in translating certain portions of the prophets. There is no way in Hebrew to distinguish between "the Lord is sending his Messiah" and "the Lord will send his Messiah." This, of course, means that it is rather risky for anyone to prove a particular theological point on the basis of the English text of the Old Testament.

A second pecularity of biblical history which makes things difficult for modern interpreters is the biblical idea that an event is simply defined as an act of God. As long as the meaning of the event, namely what God was doing therein, is clear, there is little concern with the details of the story. A good example in the Old Testament is the story of Saul's death. I Samuel 31 says clearly that Saul committed suicide by falling on his own sword. In the very next chapter (II Samuel 1) the story is told in a different way. Now it appears that Saul handed his sword to a passerby who used it to put Saul to death at his request. When we read these two stories, certain questions pop into our minds at once. Which story is correct? Obviously Saul could not have died in both of the ways described. Either one of the stories is true and the other is not, or else both of them are wrong. Another point which bothers us is why the two stories are there together. Didn't someone notice that they contradicted each other? We are left wondering whether we can believe either story.

We may simply dismiss the story of Saul's death as not being of much importance for the present-day Christian anyway. But we run into exactly the same situation when we look at the Gospel accounts of the Resurrection. Obviously, the Easter story is one of the most important events in the Bible. Yet, when we read four stories in the four Gospels we find some amazing contradictions.

Matthew (28:1-10) tells us that Mary Magdalene and another Mary went to the tomb at dawn on the first day of the week. When they arrived there was an earthquake, and an angel of the Lord descended from Heaven and rolled back the stone from the tomb and sat upon it. The women and the cemetery guards were afraid, but the angel calmed their fears and told them to share what they had seen with the disciples. As they left the tomb, Jesus met them and told them to have the disicples meet him at Galilee.

Mark (16:1-8) identifies the women who went to the tomb as Mary Magadalene, Mary the mother of James, and Salome. At once we note that there are three women in Mark's story and only two in Matthew's. Mark tells us that the stone was already rolled away when the women arrived at the tomb. There was no angel, as in Matthew's account, but a young man who was sitting *inside* the tomb. The women then left the tomb, but according to Mark's account they did not meet Jesus.

The Gospel according to Luke tells a still different story. In Luke's account (24:1-31) the three women who went to the tomb were Mary Magdalene, Mary the mother of James, and Joanna. It is suggested that other women were also there, but they are not named. Luke agrees with Mark that the stone was rolled away when the women arrived at the tomb. However, there was not one angelic figure at the tomb, but two. The women left the tomb without meeting Jesus and immediately told the disciples what they had seen. The disciples did not believe them until they themselves met Jesus near the village of Emmaus.

According to the Fourth Gospel (20:1-17), Mary Magdalene was the only woman who went to the tomb on Easter day. Seeing that the stone had already been rolled away, she ran to get the disciples and brought Simon Peter and a second disciple to the tomb. While the two disciples were in the tomb, Mary looked inside and saw two angels in white sitting where the body of Jesus had been. While she was looking in the tomb, Jesus himself appeared to her but did not tell her to have the disciples meet him in Galilee.

If we look at these stories the way that a newspaper reporter would, they simply contradict one another beyond belief. There is no agreement on the number of women present or who they were. The authors differ on whether the figures at the tomb were men or angels, and on the number that were there. The only real agreement among the four stories is in the reality of the event. It is obvious that the Christians who collected these four Gospels into one book failed to see any major contradiction in the accounts of the Resurrection. This means either that they were idiots, which is hard for us to believe, or that they didn't look at the stories in the same way that we do. The details of the event apparently made little difference to them. The important thing was what God had done in raising Jesus Christ from the dead. The attitude of the biblical writers was about the same as that of the little boy who told the story of the Exodus.[4] As long as the main point of the story, namely God's action, was made clear, there was no interest at all in the way that the event actually took place.

Because of our understanding of history, it is very difficult for us to deal with the history and narrative we find in the Bible. As we read the stories we feel frustrated over the strange ideas and practices of the writers and editors. How much simpler things would be if they had paid attention to historical detail and taken pains to get the events into the right chronological order.

Wouldn't it be interesting if we could call back one

96

of the biblical writers in the same way that Saul is said to have called Samuel back from the dead? (I Samuel 28:8-19.) Imagine how hard it would be to try to convince this ancient Hebrew that he should accept our modern definitions of "event" and "history." Eventually we might possibly persuade him to see the reasonableness of our definition and the shortcomings of his.

Suppose, though, that in the course of our discussion he were to pick up a copy of the "old" *Methodist Hymnal,* published in the 1930's. In flipping through the pages of hymns, our visitor would be delighted to find a number of poems based on Old Testament passages, particularly in the Psalms. But then, suppose he should turn to the Ritual in the back of the hymnal and find there two *contradictory* Communion services. The Hebrew would be absolutely scandalized! How could anybody publish side by side two Communion services which do not agree either in the wording of the prayers or in the order in which the prayers occur?

As a firm believer in Temple worship, this man would know that there is only one way to word a prayer. The Hebrews believed that if one or two words in a prayer were changed, its entire effectiveness would be destroyed. God expected the prayers to be worded properly and wouldn't listen to any that were not. Furthermore, a worship service had to be a meaningful *series* of prayers and hymns, not just a mixture of items with no regard to order. If the prayers were out of the proper order, then the whole meaning of the service was lost.

In order to explain the presence of two Communion rituals, side by side, we would have to explain to our Hebrew friend that our concept of ritual is quite different from his. The important thing about a prayer, we would say, is not its exact wording or details, but the relationship between God and man dramatized or brought about by this prayer. The individual words don't matter, as long as you capture the meaning of God's action in the prayer. Furthermore, it doesn't really matter what *order* the prayers follow. The important thing is what God is doing in the worship service, not the details or the order of the individual parts.

In the course of this discussion, it might dawn on us that we are both saying the same things in different ways. The difference between modern and biblical attitudes toward worship is very much like the difference between modern and biblical attitudes toward history. Eventually, it might be possible for us and our Hebrew visitor to see some meaning in each others' definitions.

On the other hand, we would still have the problem of explaining to our Hebrew friend why we have two Communion rituals in the old Hymnal, instead of just one. We would have to explain that The Methodist Church, at the time when the hymnal was published, was in the process of joining separate church groups into one church. For that reason, two rituals, each familiar to one of the merging groups, were included.

Since both rituals really contain the same thing, it didn't matter too much which one was used. Since both were included, each person could use the one he had grown up with and then everyone would be happy.

"Aha," our Hebrew friend might exclaim at this point, "I understand exactly what you mean. When the sources for the Old Testament were gathered together, we were bringing together the northern and southern Hebrew groups. The northern group had learned one story of how Saul died, and the southern group had learned another. Since both stories really said the same thing about God's relation to Saul, we put them both in the book so that each could read the story with which he was most familiar, and everyone would be satisfied."

Once again, we see that the Bible is not a book which is easily understood at first reading. Before we can understand its meaning fully, it is necessary to spend much time and effort in studying the background and culture out of which the books came. We find, however, that such study will pay huge dividends in an increased understanding of God's will for us as it is revealed in the Bible.

7 When They Begin the Begats

Have you ever read the Bible through from cover to cover, from Genesis to Revelation? I suspect that a lot of people have done it, or tried hard to do it—just once. Otherwise, we tend to settle down with the parts of the Bible we like best and never leave them. This really isn't too surprising. In going through the whole Bible, book by book, we find many sections to be rather hard reading. The priestly literature in Numbers and Leviticus, for example, looks pretty bleak and hopeless. And how about the "begats"—long lists of names, dates, and ages going on for seemingly endless generations? Then there are books like Ezekiel and Revelation whose images are so strange and complex that they stagger our understanding. How much easier it is to settle down with one of the Gospels or a handful of Psalms, with an occasional side trip into Genesis, Isaiah, or the letters of Paul! We like to stay with familiar passages, and they are familiar because they are the ones we like to read. It is difficult to find our way out of this circular pattern of Bible reading.

Believe it or not, this practice is almost as common among ministers as among laymen. Some months ago, in lecturing to a group of ministers, I accused them of using the Bible the same way they use the hymnal. Several studies in recent years show that out of all the songs in our hymnal, most ministers use only about fifty in a year's worship services. I suggested that most ministers do nearly all their preaching out of one or two Gospels, one or two books of prophecy, the Psalms, and one or two of Paul's letters.

One of the men who heard the lecture went home and dug into his records of sermons and scripture lessons used over a period of 13 years.[1] During that time, he reported later, he preached 1,878 sermons. Some 1,245 of them were from the New Testament. Only 633 were from the Old Testament. The Gospels and the book of Acts accounted for 777 sermons, or 144 more than the entire Old Testament! Almost half of the Old Testament sermons came from Genesis, Exodus, Psalms, and Isaiah. In 13 years this man had never preached on Ezra, Obadiah, the Song of Solomon, Nahum, Zepha-

101

niah, or Haggai in the Old Testament, or Philemon or II John in the New Testament.

Since much of a minister's reading is tied in with sermon preparation, I suggest that this is a good profile of the way the average minister reads the Bible. If ministers fail to deal with whole sections of the Bible, even over a ten-year period, it is not surprising that laymen are very selective in their reading.

Some sections of the Bible are so rich in meaning and challenge that the reader can spend hours on each page without drinking in all its benefit. Other sections, however, appear to be very unrewarding. With so much rich soil to till in the Bible, why should anyone try to plow the arid deserts of Leviticus and the begats?

Anyone who knows deserts can tell you that they often fool the tenderfoot. In the first place, every desert has its oases. In the middle of the most barren land imaginable, you will find a stream or spring of water which brings forth a small but lush garden. In the second place, the seemingly barren desert sands are full of life. The great Sand Dunes National Monument in Colorado has an amazing exhibit of hundreds of plants and animals which live in the apparently lifeless sand dunes. The amount of life there is unbelievable, but you have to know where and how to find it. In the third place, even a desert can be made to bloom, if cultivated in the right way. The dry desert soil is amazingly fertile when supplied with some water, skill, and hard work.

Similarly, the reader who takes time to explore the biblical deserts, such as Leviticus and the begats, will find his patience amply rewarded. Last year I was invited to visit a Christian laymen's breakfast group. Ministers (and even theological professors) were allowed if they promised not to talk, but only to listen. The group had just finished studying one of Paul's letters and was ready to begin a study of the Gospel according to Matthew. Their practice was to take one chapter each morning. After reading through the chapter, about half an hour was spent in discussing the text.

When the meeting opened, the chairman suggested that the discussion begin with the second chapter of Matthew rather than the first. He and one or two others had looked at the first 17 verses of Matthew 1 and decided they contained little of importance. Verses 18 through 25 tell the story of the announcement of Jesus' birth. This story is so familiar that there was probably little point in discussing it further. The whole group looked at the chapter for a few moments to decide whether or not to skip it.

One of the members asked whether any other Gospel gave such a list of Jesus' ancestors as Matthew 1:2-17. After a quick check, they discovered a similar list in Luke. However, it was soon obvious that the lists in Matthew and Luke did not agree on the ancestry of Joseph's father. While this fact was being discussed, another man noticed that both the genealogies traced Jesus' ancestry through Joseph rather than Mary. Why would the Gospel writers include both the ancestry of Joseph *and* the story of the Virgin Birth of Jesus? Someone else noticed that the number of generations seemed quite important to Matthew. There were fourteen generations from Abraham to David, fourteen generations from David to the Babylonian Exile, and fourteen generations from the Exile to Christ. This means that Jesus was the beginning of the *seventh seven*. This led to the discussion of the number seven as the "perfect" number throughout the Bible. Eventually, the discussion of Matthew 1:1-17 took up all the time available, and the group decided to do further research and pick up the same discussion the next week!

Some of the most powerful sermons in the Bible are found in equally unlikely places. I still remember a sermon I heard many years ago on the fifth chapter of Genesis.[2] Turn to that chapter and read through the first twenty-four verses. All you find, for verse after verse, is a monotonous list of names and dates. Each of the men listed was born, lived a certain number of years, had a son, lived a while longer, and then died. The listing is so monotonous that the reader nearly falls asleep before he gets to Enoch in verse 21.

Enoch's story starts out in exactly the same way, and then the reader is brought up short, for the end of the story is quite different. "Enoch walked with God; and he was not, for God took him." After generations and generations of men who simply lived, bore children, and died, here was a man who was different. The reason for

104

the difference in his life was his closeness to God. You can imagine how the sermon was developed, in terms of the difference that walking with God makes in a man's life today.

There are few sections of the Bible that look less rewarding than the book of Leviticus. For this reason, most casual readers of the Bible never go near it. For those who take the trouble to find it, however, there is a great deal of solid meat in the book. For example, Jesus' commandment "Love your neighbor as yourself" comes from Leviticus 19.

A closer look at this chapter reveals an amazing amount of worthwhile material. All the Ten Commandments are found there, either explicitly or implicitly. Admittedly, some of the other material looks very strange to us today. For example, farmers are forbidden to eat fruit from their trees until their fifth year of bearing. For the first three years the fruit is to be left alone. In the fourth year it must be given as an offering to God. In the fifth year and thereafter, it may be used by the owner of the tree. Unless we know the background of this passage, it looks like so much legalistic nonsense. Why shouldn't the man who owns a fruit tree be allowed to eat the fruit for three years?

The answer is closely related to verses 9 and 10 in the same chapter: "When you reap the harvest of your land, you shall not reap your field to its very border, neither shall you gather the gleanings after your harvest. And you shall not strip your vineyard bare, neither shall you gather the fallen grapes of your vineyard; you shall leave them for the poor and for the sojourner: I am the Lord your God." Those who owned vineyards, orchards, and fields had to remember that there were poor people who had no way of feeding their families. Therefore, some of each harvest was to be left for them. In the fourth year the fruit crop was given to God. This was not an arbitrary ruling, but a recognition of the fact that God was the source of every good gift. No one was allowed to forget that without God man would have nothing. Therefore, the first and best of everything was given as a thank-offering to God.

It seems amazing to us, at first, to find in the midst of all the minute points of cultic law what one scholar has called a "summary of some of the finest ethical teachings of the Old Testament, culminating in (the) injunction to love one's neighbor as one's self." [3] If we read Leviticus and other apparently unrewarding sections of the Bible, with attention to their background and purpose, we shall find that such worthwhile material is not the exception, but the rule.

Another section of the Bible almost always avoided by mainline Protestants is the so-called apocalyptic literature of the Bible, such as Daniel and Revelation. The book of Revelation (alias the Revelation of St. John the Divine) is admittedly a strange and exotic book. [4] The imagery is fanciful, unrestrained, and mysterious. Its subject is eschatology (the study of the final judgment and the end of history), admittedly a difficult area of theological concern. Because of these distinctive features, the book holds a unique place in New Testament literature.

Revelation is certainly the favorite book of one part of Protestantism. A quick check of the church page in the Saturday edition of any metropolitan paper will reveal a wide interest in its possibilities. Rarely will the pastors of certain denominations leave the book of Revelation alone, except for an occasional dip into the mysteries of Daniel, Zechariah, or Mark's "Little Apocalypse." [5] More than half of the visiting evangelists preaching in local Gospel Tabernacles will deal with one of St. John's visions in either the morning service or the evening revival hour. The sects which erect roadside signs proclaiming the immediate coming of Christ (lettered on heavy gauge steel with baked enamel finish to last for years) would be lost without phrases from Revelation.

Generally speaking, other Christians avoid the approach used by this group as they would avoid a home quarantined with smallpox. For this reason, when they pick up the book of Revelation they are embarrassed or puzzled, or both. So they skip back to another section of the Bible and do their reading there.

It would be well for us to reevaluate the importance and message of this book in terms of contemporary theology and the problems facing our churches. Although we cannot use the book of Revelation in the way that the sect groups do, it does have a message for us which cannot be ignored.

The first three chapters of the book present few problems. The letters to the seven churches of Asia sound modern enough to have been written by any denominational executive to any local congregation. Any of us could give current examples of the church that "has the name of being alive, but is dead," and the church which is "neither hot nor cold, but luke-warm." All that is needed to apply this material to our situation is a certain amount of courage.

The other nineteen chapters, however, pose real problems. In the first place, the imagery is so complex and difficult that a thorough explanation of the meaning is nearly impossible. In the second place, we have learned not to use Revelation as a blueprint for world history or a basis for predicting the future. In the third place, our theology today is quite different than that of the author of the book.

An understanding of the meaning of Revelation for our day requires knowledge of its background. Shortly after A.D. 90, all residents of the Roman empire were required to worship a statue of the Emperor Domitian or face a death sentence. Christian leaders divided into two camps over the issue. One group insisted on a flat refusal to commit idolatry, no matter what the con-sequences. The other group recommended a com-promise, suggesting that Christians *pretend* to worship the statue in order to stay alive. Otherwise all Christians in the Empire would be executed, and no one would remain to preach the Gospel.

The book of Revelation was written to challenge the latter position. It maintained that compromise is *not* a Christian option. The argument that compromise is legitimate if it preserves a system or institution in which the Gospel is preached is thrown out. The author reminds us that the Author of the universe and the Lord of the church is still the Lord of history. The responsibility of the Christian is to remain faithful to God, not to preserve the church as it is. If a faithful witness requires individual martyrdom and even the destruction of the church as we know it, God is still capable of carrying out his plans for his world. The message of the book of Revelation is still desperately needed today. The statue of Domitian is no longer an issue, but worship of the status quo is!

It goes without saying that in such difficult and less familiar passages of the Bible, the nonspecialist will lean very heavily on outside resources for help in understanding the material. It is also true that commentaries and other reference books can be of great help in reading the *rest* of the Bible. Those who have had at least a college course in Bible are usually able to find their way around in the book without great difficulty. For those with no background in biblical history, it is easy to become lost in a whirl of unfamiliar names, dates, places, and events. Those who have tried to read the Old Testament without knowing its background will appreciate the comment of a friend of mine that he enjoys reading the Old Testament but has never been able to figure out its plot!

The book of Acts tells of an Ethiopian riding from Jerusalem to Gaza, reading from the Old Testament as he went (Acts 8:26-39). The disciple Phillip, seeing that the man was reading the book of Isaiah, asked him "Do you understand what you are reading?" "How can I," replied the Ethiopian, "unless someone guides me?" The same question might well be asked by the interested layman today. Even though the book of Isaiah is quite familiar to most church members, its use is much more fruitful after a study of its background and composition.

The book as we have it is a combination of three different books. Chapters 1 through 39 contain mainly the work of Isaiah of Jerusalem, a prophet whose ministry extended from 742 B.C. to about 695. Chapters 40 through 55 are mainly the work of a sixth century B.C. prophet who probably accompanied the Hebrews in their return from the Babylonian exile about 520-515 B.C. Chapters 56 through 66 are a collection of poetry and prose, probably from the fifth century B.C. Even within I Isaiah (chapters 1-39) the material is arranged by subject, rather than chronology. Chapter 1 probably reflects the attack of Sennacherib on Jerusalem in 701 B.C. Chapter 2 contains a quotation from the fourth chapter of Micah, and most of it probably comes from the period after the Exile. Chapter 5 comes from the early ministry of Isaiah, probably shortly after 740 B.C. Chapter 6 deals with Isaiah's call to become a prophet in the year King Uzziah died, which was 742. Chapter 7 deals with the Syro-Ephraimitic War, about 734 B.C. Chapter 10 probably was written after 717 B.C. Without a commentary, a reading of these 10 chapters may simply lead to confusion!

For the layman who wants to get the most from his Bible reading, many excellent resources are available.[6] For many years the best standard commentary for layman was the *Abingdon Bible Commentary*. First published in 1929, it is still of some value, although many sections are badly out of date. For those who can afford it, *The Interpreter's Bible* is a good twelve-volume commentary. It includes the Revised Standard and King James texts of the Old and New Testaments, with introductory articles, a detailed explanation of each passage, and an application of the text to the problems of today's world. Both *The Interpreter's Bible* and *The Interpreter's Dictionary of the Bible* are excellent reference sets for church libraries or adult church school classes. The latter set is, in my opinion, the best general Bible reference work published in English in this century. Additional resources for Bible study will be found listed in the bibliography at the end of this book.

One of the first questions the reader has to decide before beginning a serious program of Bible reading is which translation to read. If the Bible on your shelf is ten years old or more, it is probably a King James translation. Without doubt this is one of the most beautiful pieces of literature in the English language. No translation before or since has matched it for poetic beauty. For personal devotions or public worship, its beauty is unmatched. However, for study purposes it has several drawbacks. In the first place, when the translation was made in 1611 there were few good manuscripts of the Greek New Testament available. Since that time, scholars have discovered many excellent manuscripts, going back as far as the second century A.D. In the second place, many of the words in the King James Bible have changed their meaning since the seventeenth century. Others have simply dropped out of ordinary English usage.[7]

On several occasions, the King James Bible has been revised by competent and dedicated teams of scholars. The most recent of these revisions is the Revised Standard Version Bible, published since World War II. The New Testament first appeared in 1946, the Old Testament in 1952, and the Apocrypha in 1957. This translation has kept the rhythm and wording of the King James translation whenever possible, but has removed the problems noted in the previous paragraph. It is especially popular among those who love the language of the King James but want to be able to understand the text thoroughly. Since the RSV translation first appeared, there have been several excellent study Bibles based on it. The best is the *Westminster Study Bible* published by Collins Press. It provides the reader with helpful background material through introductory articles and numerous footnotes. Another good resource is the *Oxford Annotated RSV*, published by Oxford University Press. It provides similar background and information, although its scholarship is much more conservatively oriented.

The RSV translation is entirely an American project. The British, instead of producing a new revision of the King James Bible, preferred to produce a new English translation from the ground up. Because of the war, they were unable to begin this *New English Bible* project until 1947. The New Testament translation of the NEB appeared in 1960. It is hoped that the Old Testament will be finished and published shortly after 1970. Presumably, this will be followed by the NEB Apocrypha.

The *New English Bible* is an exciting, fresh translation which will appeal particularly to young people. The reasons given by the translations committee for this New English version are threefold. In the first place, they wanted to reach the many millions of people "who have no effective contact with any of the churches," for whom the King James is completely unfamiliar. Secondly, this translation was designed to be used in schools where the Bible is studied as a part of the history of culture. Thirdly, there are many people who know the King James translation so well that they no longer pay attention to what the words say. In reading a new translation, they may be jolted out of their familiar pattern and forced to take the text seriously. The only difficulty with the New English Bible for American readers is that it has a somewhat British flavour!

The King James, Revised Standard Version, and New English Bible were all produced by committees of scholars. Several translations available today were produced by individual translators. Many people prefer these translations because of their fresh, exciting phrasing. It must be remembered, however, that individual translators can be irresponsible. Because they do not have to answer to other scholars, they often slant the text so that only *their* interpretation comes through. The best example of this combination of exciting language and unacceptable slanting is the work of J. B. Phillips.

Reading the Bible is seldom easy, but it is infinitely rewarding. It can be done on several levels—for pleasure, devotional purposes, or instruction. No one can tell someone else how to read it, except to say that any reader should open himself fully to its challenge and be willing and ready to respond to its call.

8 Truly I
Say unto You

By now it should be apparent that biblical scholarship is a broad and a complex field. In fact, it is not a single field at all, but a combination of several related disciplines. Not even a professional can expect to know all these fields in detail. However, a quick survey of their scope should be helpful to anyone beginning serious Bible study.

Chapter 2, "How Did the Bible Happen?" has already provided a glimpse into the study of the Bible as *literature*. In college, an English literature major can study the Bible in the same way he studies seventeenth-century poetry or medieval drama. Each book is analyzed in terms of style, date, authorship, and content. In some cases, comparison with the literature of other cultures is helpful. For example, there is a Babylonian story about a worldwide flood survived by only one family on an ark, and an Egyptian story about a man like Job. There are also stories from Mesopotamia which closely resemble parts of the Creation stories in Genesis. Study of this literature helps us to see sources from which details of biblical stories may have been drawn. However, such research also points up the unique spiritual quality of the Bible. In the Egyptian and Mesopotamian stories there are always several gods, jealous of each other and fighting among themselves. In one story, one god kills another and forms the world from the dead body. Only in the Bible do we find one God, ruler of the whole universe, who creates the world and mankind out of love and concern. In other eastern religions man is supposed to fear the gods and has to bribe them to have mercy on him. In the Old Testament, God creates man for fellowship with him.

Obviously, the comparison of the Bible with other ancient literature requires a knowledge of several dead *languages*. A century ago very few ancient Near Eastern languages were understood or even known. Then, excavations in Mesopotamia began to turn up hundreds of inscribed tablets. By 1900 scholars had figured out the language patterns and could read these texts. Not only have these documents shed new light on the Old Testament, but such languages as Akkadian and Ugaritic have led scholars to a deeper understanding of Hebrew.[1] Old Testament words whose meanings are obscure can sometimes be traced to a known root in another Semitic language.[2]

In recent years our knowledge of New Testament Greek has also been increased by the work of biblical linguists. The language of the New Testament is not like either classical Greek of the period of Plato, or modern Greek. It was once thought that "Bible Greek" was an invention of the Holy Spirit, just for the writing of the New Testament. This idea was used as an argument for the literal verbal inspiration of the text. In recent years, however, excavations have turned up hundreds of legal and business documents from the first century A.D. They prove that New Testament Greek was the common language of the Hellenistic period all over the Mediterranean world. In many cases these secular manuscripts have enriched our understanding of the New Testament language. For example, the word translated "meek" in Matthew 5:5 was used to refer to a wild horse which had been "broken to the saddle." Thus, the word "disciplined" would be better than "meek," especially since the latter often means "weak" or "mild" in common usage. Many of the biblical insights of linguistic study are now available to the layman in new translations and in recent Bible dictionaries.

Much of the progress in biblical linguistic study has been made possible by *archaeology*. In the past century the work of the archaeologist has changed almost completely. He used to be a collector of artifacts for museums, poking around ancient sites with the help of a few local workmen. Now he is a scientist who uses the latest discoveries of physics and chemistry to help rewrite ancient history.

Before beginning an excavation, the archaeologist identifies his buried city and, from literary sources, becomes an expert on its history. Usually an ancient mound will contain not one but several cities, each one built on the remains of the last. As each layer is removed, careful records are kept of all articles found. Jewelry, implements, coins, and even broken pieces of pottery can be used to date each layer of occupation. Surveyors, artists, and photographers preserve all the evidence for later generations of scholars to study. In recent years the most modern scientific tools, such as radio-carbon dating tests, have been made available to archaeologists. The latest development on the drawing board, believe it or not, is the use of satellite photography to identify new sites—even under water!

On the basis of archaeological work and newly discovered documents, such as the Dead Sea Scrolls, the history of the ancient Near East is gradually being pieced together like a giant jigsaw puzzle. Each summer further excavations provide new pieces to be fitted into the picture. The more complete the picture, the better we can understand the Old and New Testaments in terms of their contexts.

Fully as important as historical context, for the biblical scholar, is the *reconstruction of the original text* of the various books. No original manuscript of any book of the Bible still exists. The best manuscripts available today are about 200 to 1,500 years later than the original writings. At present we know of more than 3,000 Greek manuscripts containing part or all of the New Testament. They range in age from about A.D. 150 to the late Middle Ages. From this mass of material the original text of the New Testament must be reconstructed, even though no two of these manuscripts agree in every detail. For well over a century textual scholars have poured over the evidence, patiently comparing the variant readings. In recent years all the available knowledge on the subject has been fed into computers, which are speeding up the process immeasurably.

The original text of the Old Testament is a particular concern of scholars today. Twenty-five years ago most of the problems in this field had been solved. Then the Dead Sea discoveries provided us with manuscripts one thousand years older than any previously known. Since some of these scrolls have not even been made available for study yet, it will be at least fifty years before their total effect on biblical scholarship will become apparent.[3]

After the work of the linguists, archaeologists, historians, textual scholars, and other technical experts has been done, there still remains the task of *interpreting the text*. The various branches of critical scholarship take the Bible apart to examine each piece carefully.

Then it is the task of the biblical theologian to put it back together again. Only in this way can the meaning of the text in terms of today's world be determined. As the interpreter works with the biblical text, he brings to his task the same combination of individual personality and guidance of the Holy Spirit which we see in the writing of the books themselves.

Now that we have surveyed, all too briefly, the various areas of biblical research and the contributions of each, let us turn to some practical suggestions for the layman's study of the Bible today. It is best to study in groups, whenever possible. You will find that sharing your reactions to a passage will often help to make its meaning clearer for everyone. Large gatherings are all right for introductory lectures, but discussion seems to take place best in groups of six to ten or twelve people. The group may contain a resource person who has had some formal biblical training, such as a pastor, but this is by no means a necessity. If no resource person is available for individual groups, it may be wise to gather several groups together at first for some lectures by a specialist, which can set the stage for group discussions.

Once study groups are established, they should meet regularly. In most cases an hour a week or two hours every other week seems to be a good schedule. The group cannot function properly unless all the members keep faith with the schedule. Some of the most successful groups have agreed to attend every session except for emergencies of the sort that would cause them to miss work.

Since it takes some time for a group to jell, the course of study should be spread out over several months. Some groups begin meeting in September or October and continue until May. Others prefer to have one study project for fall and winter and another for spring and early summer. It is important to decide at an early date what section of the Bible is to be covered and what resources are to be used.

The success of any study group will depend largely on the advance preparation of the members. An unprepared group simply engages in a pooling of ignorance. Each member of the group should read carefully the passage of scripture to be discussed. One person per session may be designated to do some research on the background of the passage. An even better method is to have every member buy or borrow a good commentary or Bible dictionary and be responsible for its material each session. Sometimes it is helpful to have various members of the group use different translations, for purposes of comparison. A group member who reads a foreign language well might find a translation in that language interesting for comparison. A list of helpful resources will be found in the bibliography, beginning on page 133.

The amount of material to be covered in each session will have to be determined by the group, through experience. On some evenings a chapter or two will be covered. On other occasions a single verse will require two hours of discussion.

It is always important to choose a good starting place. Generally, it is better not to begin with Genesis. Many groups have found the best starting place to be one of Paul's letters. One group read Galatians first, then Colossians, I and II Corinthians, then Mark, John, and finally the Old Testament, beginning with the prophets Amos and Micah.

As a study group moves from one book to another, it is important to set each in its historical context. If you hear one or two phrases from a political speech, it is hard to evaluate and understand them until you know who said them, where, when, and under what circumstances. The same is true of biblical materials. Each group should develop a checklist of questions to set new material in context. Who was the author? Who made up the original audience? What was the occasion? What is the overall plan of the book? How does each individual section fit into that plan?

The serious study of the Bible, whether done alone or as part of a group, can be one of the most revealing experiences of Christian life for anyone who will open himself to its truth. The Bible, as we have said before, is the record of God's search for man. God created man in his own image so that man might have fellowship with him. From the beginning, God has sought man out and tried to draw him into this fellowship. Man was given dominion over the world and was allowed to use everything in it for his own benefit. The only restriction put upon him was that he not forget his Creator. As long as man recognized God as the source of his life and the Lord of nature, he was allowed to do nearly anything he wished.

Man, however, was unwilling to accept his responsibility to God. Instead of acknowledging God as Creator and Lord of the universe, he tried to take for himself the prerogatives of God. Man's pride and willful disobedience are demonstrated in the stories of the Garden of Eden (Genesis 3) and the Tower of Babel (Genesis 11). Dismayed at man's refusal to acknowledge and serve him, God sought him out to reestablish the fellowship which had been broken by man's sin. However, man seemed as determined to avoid God as God was to seek him out.

In due time God commissioned a series of prophets to bring his message to mankind. These men reminded their countrymen of God's claim upon them and called them back to the fellowship with God for which they had been created. The story of the prophets' lives is a gloomy one indeed. At best, the people ignored the message they brought. At worst, they ridiculed the prophets and persecuted them, sometimes even to the point of death.

Finally, God despaired of simply sending messengers and decided to involve himself completely in the lives of his people. He entered human history in the person of Jesus of Nazareth, so that the Creator of the universe became one with his creation.

Those who knew Jesus Christ and responded to him found themselves in a new relationship with God and the world. When they experienced in Christ the Creator's power and the true meaning of the universe, they were unable to explain exactly what had happened to them, but they were able to testify that their experience of Christ had given them a new kind of existence. Now they understood what it meant to be fully human. The world no longer controlled them, but could now be used as a means of achieving their true potential and of serving God.

The Christian church grew out of the fellowship of those who had known Christ and experienced a new life through that knowledge. The members of this fellowship spread throughout the world the good news (gospel) of what had happened to them. Strangely enough, those who had never met Christ in person seemed to have a genuine experience of meeting him as they heard the testimony of his disciples.

After a time, as we have seen in Chapter 2, the testimony of the church concerning this gospel was put into written form. The written testimony of the good news served the same function as the spoken testimony. As people read the Bible within the fellowship of the church, they were led into an experience with God as revealed in Jesus Christ. As they learned of the Christ event, they themselves received and responded to the challenge which the disciples had known. They met Christ, the *Living Word,* through the testimony of him in the *written word* of the Bible.

Throughout the centuries the Bible has been a means of leading men into encounter with Christ. As the generations have passed, however, it has become more difficult for men to understand this message in its own terms. In his teaching, Jesus used images with which listeners were familiar. His parables dealt with fishermen, tax collectors, herdsmen, and farmers. Today in an urban society few of us have direct knowledge of the images Jesus used. Furthermore, as we have seen, the Bible was written in a prescientific age. This raises a barrier for those who think and speak scientifically when they read the biblical text. The very images and thought forms which once helped to communicate the biblical message now make it difficult for twentieth-century man to understand.

The Bible is still the Word of God. Its message is still capable of lifting a man out of himself into a new relationship with God. However, we cannot assume that this will happen automatically if the church simply lays a seventeenth-century English translation in front of a sophisticated twentieth-century man and then walks away. The Gideon Bible in the hotel room may be a helpful gesture, but it doesn't go far enough. Even if the maid opens it on the dresser and the tired executive picks it up, he may find only frustration in the quaint language and the stories of demons, angels, and four-headed beasts. He may well turn away in dismay and give up on the Bible entirely, before ever finding its truth.

There was a time when King James English and stories of angels stirred recollections of Sunday school training and reopened doors which had been shut for years. Today, for a large percentage of the population, this process doesn't work because the recollections are simply not there.

Today new methods must be used to guide the searcher into the realities of the Bible and to challenge the "couldn't care less" type to take it seriously. We are using the most modern and efficient methods now in church construction, organization, and communication. The church has invested in high-speed presses, computers, and closed-circuit television to improve our communication of the gospel. In the light of this, we can hardly afford a medieval attitude toward the Bible!

We have now provided new translations of the text which are readable and clear. We must also take seriously the culture gap between the first and twentieth centuries. When we face it honestly, we can overcome it so that the truth of the Bible shines through.

The truth of the Bible, with its power for renewal, is our birthright. We must not make the mistake of Esau and sell that birthright for a mess of pottage! We cannot afford to worship the Bible instead of trying to understand it and respond to its challenge. We cannot afford to protect it from the challenge of the twentieth century, so that its message for our age is strangled and muted. We cannot substitute a sterile biblical literalism for an acceptance of the personal and social demands of the gospel.

In studying the Bible today, our question is for its truth and the fulfillment of what the truth demands of us. What is the truth of the Bible? It is none other than Jesus Christ; God in our midst. In his own words, Christ is the way, the *truth,* and the life.

"If you continue in my word," Jesus said, "you are truly my disciples, and you will have the truth, and the truth will make you free." This phrase is often quoted and usually misunderstood. The "truth" referred to has been incorrectly identified as Gnosticism, scientism, Aristotelianism, Marxism, capitalism, theosophy, theocracy, and a host of other "answers." In context, the truth referred to is Christ himself. If we know him, through the word which testifies to him and the church which is his Body, we shall be free indeed.

Notes

1. The Book Few People Know

1. For further discussion on this point see the preface to the Revised Standard Version of the Bible.
2. For a list of available translations, see the bibliography.
3. Compare Genesis 1:1 through 2:4a with 2:4b-23.
4. A concordance is a list of all the words in the Bible, in alphabetical order, with a reference to each place the word appears. For a listing of concordances and Bible dictionaries, see the bibliography.
5. Author's translation. The word "scripture" in this context refers to the Hebrew Bible, our Old Testament.

2. How Did the Bible Happen?

1. It was unusual but not unique to find a woman functioning as a prophet. Other examples in the Bible are Deborah

(Judges 4:4) and Anna (Luke 2:36). The text does not indicate why Huldah was chosen to pass judgment on the book.

2. The King did take the book seriously. The result was a religious upheaval called the "Josianic" or "Deuteronomic" Reformation. The term *Deuteronomion* is Greek for "second law" (the ten commandments being the "first law").

3. This date and those for the canonization of the other two sections of the Old Testament are only approximate.

4. For a description of this process, see any good introduction to Old Testament literature, e.g. N. K. Gottwald, *A Light to the Nations* (New York: Harper & Row, 1959) pp. 273-81.

5. See R. J. Williams' article on "Writing" in *The Interpreter's Dictionary of the Bible*, IV, 909-21.

6. See II Samuel 8:15-17.

7. The name means "hidden (books)." These books are I and II Esdras, Tobit, Judith, the additions to Esther, the Wisdom of Solomon, Ecclesiasticus, Baruch, the Letter of Jeremiah, the additions to Daniel, the Prayer of Manasseh, and I and II Maccabees. They were retained in the canon of the Christian church in the 1st century A.D. Martin Luther later removed them from his canon, and Protestants have generally followed his lead.

8. For a discussion of the problems involved in dating Jesus' birth, see C. Milo Connick, *Jesus* (Englewood Cliffs, New Jersey: Prentice Hall, 1963), pp. 107-109.

9. The one-year ministry is obvious, on the basis of the accounts of Matthew, Mark, and Luke. The three-year tradition is based on the three passover references in John. The Synoptic Gospels are probably more reliable at this point.

10. There is general agreement among New Testament scholars that Paul wrote Romans, I and II Corinthians, Galatians, Philippians, I Thessalonians, and Philemon. There is considerable disagreement on the authorship of II Thessalonians,

Colossians, and Ephesians. Most scholars feel that I and II Timothy, Titus, and Hebrews were written long after Paul's death.

11. For further information on John Mark, see E. P. Blair's article in *The Interpreter's Dictionary of the Bible*, III, 277-78.

12. This source is simply called "Q"—an abbreviation of the German word "Quelle," meaning "source."

13. See John 19:28-34.

14. For a listing and a discussion of these books, see M. S. Enslin's article "Apocrypha, N. T." in *The Interpreter's Dictionary of the Bible*, I, 166-69.

15. Marcion was a Gnostic. Any good encyclopedia will give further information on his life and work.

16. The list of the accepted New Testament books was never published officially until the Council of Trent in the 16th century.

3. Facts and Fiction

1. Uriah, who was a Hittite rather than a Hebrew, was apparently a mercenary in David's army.

2. In sparsely settled desert areas, any traveler is entitled to food and lodging for the asking, even if he is a stranger.

3. It was the Assyrians who destroyed the nation of Israel about 721 B.C. and deported most of the population for resettlement. This marked the end of the ten northern tribes of Israel, thereafter called the "Ten Lost Tribes." Only Judah and the priestly tribe of Levi remained.

4. For a further discussion of this point, see B. D. Rahtjen, *Scripture and Social Action* (Nashville: Abingdon Press, 1966) pp. 18-37.

5. This definition is taken from Rudolf Bultmann. See his *Jesus Christ and Mythology* (New York: Charles Scribner's Sons, 1958) esp. Chap. 1.

6. For the biblical definitions of "Heaven" see T. H. Gaster's article in *The Interpreter's Dictionary of the Bible*, II, 551-52.
7. See Bultmann, *Jesus Christ and Mythology*, Chap. 3, for a full discussion of demythologizing.

4. Science and/or Religion

1. The following definitions of inductive and deductive reasoning have been oversimplified for purposes of comparison. Any good dictionary of philosophy can be consulted for a more complete discussion.

5. What About Miracles?

1. Quintus Septimus Florens Tertullianus (Tertullian), born A.D. 160.
2. Compare, for example, Mark 6:30-44 and Mark 8:1-9.
3. In the following section of this chapter, I am indebted to some of R. H. Fuller's suggestions in *Interpreting the Miracles* (Philadelphia: The Westminster Press, 1963).

6. History Then and Now

1. Even the *names* of events change. For example, was it the "Civil War" or the "War Between the States"?
2. See above, p. 67.
3. The terms "perfect" form (completed) and "imperfect" form (incomplete) are sometimes used.
4. See above, p. 82.

7. When They Begin the Begats

1. At this point, I am indebted to the Rev. William Wilder of the North Arkansas Conference of The United Methodist Church.
2. The preacher was the Rev. Raymond E. Neff, who was my District Superintendent in the Newark Conference, 1958–60.

3. *Westminster Study Bible*—RSV (New York: Collins, 1965), p. 156. Scholars preparing the footnotes are not specifically identified by name.
4. In this discussion, I have borrowed heavily on an article I published in the *Christian Advocate*, Vol. 8, no. 12, entitled "Revelation: a Lost Book." Quotations from that article are incorporated here, with permission of the copyright holder.
5. Mark 13.
6. For full information on publishers, dates, etc., see the bibliography at the end of this volume.
7. These points are discussed at length in the preface to the Revised Standard Version. Note also p. 13, above.

8. Truly I Say unto You

1. Akkadian was the Semitic language of early settlers in Mesopotamia. The Assyrians and Babylonians spoke dialects of it. Ugaritic was the language of the Canaanites who inhabited Palestine before the Hebrew conquest. It is also Semitic.
2. There are many such words which appear only once in the Old Testament and nowhere else in Hebrew literature. The book of Job is full of them.
3. Many of the scrolls found by individual Arabs were purchased with museum endowment funds. The manuscripts cannot be released for translation and publication until these funds have been reimbursed. It is not true, as some have charged, that these manuscripts have been withheld for theological reasons.

Bibliography

Basic Reference Works

Buttrick, George (ed.). *The Interpreter's Bible*. Nashville: Abingdon Press, 1951-57. 12 volumes.

Probably the most common commentary in use today. It gives the KJV and RSV on the same page, with explanatory notes and sermon ideas. Some parts are excellent, others very poor. Some of it is already out of date. Helpful in a church library for comparison with other commentaries. Not recommended for purchase by individuals.

——— (ed.). *The Interpreter's Dictionary of the Bible*. Nashville: Abingdon Press, 1962. 4 volumes. The best Bible dictionary available in English. Every church library should have one if possible. For churches that want to start a reference library, this is the best purchase with which to begin.

Concordance to the Revised Standard Version. New York: Thomas Nelson & Sons, 1961.

Cruden, Alexander. *Cruden's Complete Concordance to the Bible* (KJV). First published in 1737. Now available in several editions.

Gospel Parallels. New York: Thomas Nelson & Sons, 1949.
A synopsis of the first three Gospels. Lists Matthew, Mark, and Luke in parallel columns on each page for purposes of comparative study. No study of the Gospels should be done without it.

Metzger, B. M. and I. M. *The Oxford Concise Concordance to the Revised Standard Version of the Holy Bible.* New York: Oxford University Press, 1962.
An inexpensive concordance of only 158 pages which is designed for the average reader. A much better investment for an individual than the full RSV concordance.

Miller, M. S., and J. L. *Harper's Bible Dictionary.* New York: Harper & Row, 1952.
A good one-volume reference work. Somewhat out of date, now.

Richardson, Alan (ed.). *A Theological Wordbook of the Bible.* New York: The Macmillan Company, 1950.
Now available in paperback. An excellent reference work for group discussion purposes.

Modern Translations

New English Bible (New Testament only). Oxford: Oxford University Press; Cambridge: Cambridge University Press, 1961.
Available in several editions, including inexpensive paperbacks.

Schonfield, Hugh J. (trans.). *The Authentic New Testament.* New York: Mentor Books, 1958.

Paperback. One of the best literal translations of the New Testament ever done, though Mr. Schonfield is a Jewish scholar.

Commentaries and Study Editions of the Bible

Albright, W. F., and Freedman, D. N. (eds.). *The Anchor Bible.* Garden City, N. Y. : Doubleday & Co. 38 volumes.
This rather high-priced set is being published at the rate of three or four volumes per year. Each volume has an excellent new translation of one or more books of the Bible. The introductions and footnotes are too technical to be of much help to laymen.

Barclay, William, and Bruce, F. F. (eds.). *Bible Guides.* Nashville: Abingdon Press.
A series of 22 paperbacks, giving introductions to all the books of the Bible. Simple and easy to read, yet they deal with most of the important critical issues. They make good textbooks for group study. The authors are all excellent scholars.

Dillistone, F. W., *et al.* (eds.). *Westminster Study Bible* (RSV). New York: Collins Clear-Type Press, 1965.
The best study Bible available in English. Excellent introductory material and explanatory footnotes.

Eiselen, F. C., Lewis, Edwin, and Downey, D. G. *The Abingdon Bible Commentary.* Nashville: Abingdon Press, 1929.
Once an excellent reference work. Now very badly out of date.

Jones, Alexander (ed.). *The Jerusalem Bible.* Garden City, N. Y.: Doubleday & Co., 1966.
This English translation of the Bible is one of the best. The introductory material and footnotes are dated and heavily slanted toward a pre-Vatican II Roman Catholic point of view. Available as a whole Bible or as a separate New Testament. Expensive.

May, H. G., and Metzger, B. M. *The Oxford Annotated Bible* (RSV). New York: Oxford University Press, 1962.
A good study Bible in general. The notes on the New Testament section are weighted toward a very conservative viewpoint.

Metzger, B. M. (ed.). *The Oxford Annotated Apocrypha.* New York: Oxford University Press, 1965.
The best study edition of the Old Testament Apocrypha.

Rad, G. von. *Genesis: A Commentary.* Philadelphia: Westminster Press, 1961. This is the first (and best) of the new "Old Testament Library" series being published by Westminster Press in the U.S. and SCM Press in England. Most of the volumes are translations of the work of German scholars. When completed, this will be one of the best sets of Old Testament commentaries in English. This would be an excellent reference set for a church library. Other volumes in the series already published are *Exodus* (M. Noth), *Leviticus* (M. Noth), *Deuteronomy* (G. von Rad) *I and II Samuel* (H. W. Hertzberg), *I and II Kings* (J. Gray), *Psalms* (A. Weiser) and *Daniel* (N. Porteous.)

Studies in the Old Testament

Anderson, B. W. *Understanding the Old Testament.* 2nd ed. Englewood Cliffs, N. J.: Prentice-Hall, 1966.
Written for use as a college textbook in Old Testament.

Eissfeldt. Otto. *The Old Testament: An Introduction.* New York: Harper & Row, 1965.
The definitive reference book on Old Testament scholarship during the past century.

Hebert, Gabriel. *The Old Testament from Within.* New York: Oxford University Press, 1962.
Historical and theological survey of the Old Testament. Paperback.

136

Napier, B. D. *Song of the Vineyard*. New York: Harper & Row, 1962.
Written in an interesting style.

Rowley, H. H. *The Old Testament and Modern Study*. New York: Oxford University Press, 1950.
The history of Old Testament scholarship, 1900-1950.

Sarna, Nahum. *Understanding Genesis*. New York: McGraw-Hill, 1967.
The first of a new series of Jewish commentaries on the Old Testament, designed primarily for teachers in synagogue schools. An excellent resource to present a traditional Jewish viewpoint on the Bible. Later volumes in the series should be worth reading.

Weiser, Artur. *The Old Testament: Its Formation and Development*. New York: Association Press, 1961.
An excellent reference book, but not easy to read.

Studies in the New Testament

Connick, C. Milo. *Jesus: The Man, the Mission, and the Message*, Englewood Cliffs, N. J.: Prentice-Hall, 1963.
A good college-level text.

Grant, F. C. *The Gospels*. New York: Harper & Brothers, 1957.
A good discussion of the background of the Gospels and the relationships among them.

Kee, H. C., Young, F. W., and Froelich, K. *Understanding the New Testament*. Englewood Cliffs, N. J.: Prentice-Hall, 1966.
A good college-level New Testament textbook.

Klassen, W., and Snyder, G. *Current Issues in New Testament Interpretation*. New York: Harper & Row, 1962.
A survey of recent New Testament scholarship. Fairly technical.

Kümmel, W. G. (ed.). *Introduction to the New Testament*. Nashville: Abingdon Press, 1966.

The latest edition of the most famous German introduction to the study of the New Testament. Still the best reference book on the New Testament ever written. The footnotes give a complete listing of important New Testament scholarship for the past 100 years.

Lace, O. J. (ed.). *Understanding the New Testament.* Cambridge, England: The University Press, 1965.

Introductory volume to the *New Cambridge Bible Commentary on the New English Bible.* A good history of the New Testament against its historical background. This commentary is a good one for laymen and is being published in paperback, a few volumes at a time. Well worth having.

Nock, A. D. *St. Paul.* New York: Harper & Row, 1937. Now available in paperback (Torchbook No. 104). A good introduction to Paul's life and letters.

Patterson, C. H. *New Testament Notes.* Lincoln, Neb.: Cliff's Notes, Inc., 1965.

Those who have used Cliff's Notes in college will recognize this outline series. This is an excellent study outline for the New Testament.

Saunders, E. W. *Jesus in the Gospels.* Englewood Cliffs, N. J.: Prentice-Hall, 1967.

A good recent study of what can be known of Jesus of Nazareth.

Background Materials and Other Special Studies Related to the Bible

Albright, W. F. *The Archaeology of Palestine.* Baltimore: Penguin Books (A199), 1961.

Paperback. Gives the history of Biblical archaeology in an easy to understand form.

Baly, Denis. *The Geography of the Bible.* New York: Harper & Row, 1957.

A good secondary reference work.

138

Bright, John. *A History of Israel*. Philadelphia: Westminster Press, 1959.

The best single-volume Old Testament history now available.

Burrows, Millar. *The Dead Sea Scrolls*. New York: Viking Press, 1955.

The best original study of the earliest Dead Sea Scrolls, with English translations of the texts.

————*More Light on the Dead Sea Scrolls*. New York: Viking Press, 1958.

A worthy companion to Burrows' first volume on the Dead Sea Scrolls. Both are now classics in their field.

Chiera, Edward. *They Wrote on Clay*. Chicago: University of Chicago Press, 1938.

Available in paperback (Phoenix P2). A well written account of Mesopotamian life during the Old Testament period.

Farb, Peter. *The Land, Wildlife, and Peoples of the Bible*. New York: Harper & Row, 1967.

A well written discussion of the land of Palestine by a leading naturalist. Good background reading.

Fuller, Reginald. *Interpreting the Miracles*. Philadelphia: Westminster Press, 1963.

Further discussion of some of the ideas presented in Chapter 6.

Gaster, T. H. *The Dead Sea Scriptures*. Garden City, N. Y.: Doubleday & Co. (Anchor A92), 1957.

Greenslade, S. L. (ed.). *The Cambridge History of the Bible: The West from the Reformation to the Present Day*. Cambridge, England: The University Press, 1963.

The history of biblical scholarship for the past 400 years. A good resource for those who want to read further on issues raised in this book.

Habgood, John. *Truths in Tension: New Perspectives on Re-*

ligion and Science. New York: Holt, Rinehart & Winston, 1965.

A good study by a research scientist who is also a clergyman.

Kenyon, Sir Frederic. *Our Bible and the Ancient Manuscripts.* 5th ed. New York: Harper & Row, 1958.

A detailed study of the use of ancient manuscripts to reestablish the original Greek and Hebrew texts.

Miller, M. S., and J. L. *Encyclopedia of Bible Life.* New York: Harper & Row, 1944.

Good, but a bit out of date.

Pfeiffer, Robert H. *History of New Testament Times: With an Introduction to the Apocrypha.* New York: Harper & Row, 1949.

A good reference book.

Rahtjen, B. D. *Scripture and Social Action.* Nashville: Abingdon Press, 1966.

Shows how the Bible directs the church in its twofold task of evangelism and social action.

Reumann, J. H. P. *The Romance of Bible Scripts and Scholars.* Englewood Cliffs, N. J. : Prentice-Hall, 1965.

A popular but scholarly account of the use of ancient manuscripts by biblical scholars. A delight to read—almost like a historical novel.

Snaith, Norman. *The Jews from Cyrus to Herod.* Nashville: Abingdon Press, 1956.

A good historical survey of the intertestamental period.

Thomas, D. W. (ed.) . *Documents from Old Testament Times.* New York: Harper & Row (Torchbook TB85) , 1961.

A good selection of ancient Near Eastern documents contemporary with the Bible.

Toombs, L. E. *God's People Among the Nations.* New York: Association Press, 1963.

Paperback. Sets Old Testament history in its overall context.

Index